SUPERSIZE MAD LIBS

Mad Libs
An Imprint of Penguin Random House

MAD LIBS
An Imprint of Penguin Random House LLC, New York

Ⓟ

Concept created by Roger Price & Leonard Stern

Photo credits: cat: (cover, pages 49, 55-95): GlobalP/Thinkstock;
dog: (cover, pages 145, 151-191): Eric Isselée/Thinkstock.

Supersize Mad Libs published in 2017 by Mad Libs,
an imprint of Penguin Random House LLC, New York.
Printed in the USA.

Visit us online at www.penguinrandomhouse.com.

Supersize Mad Libs ISBN 9781524785062

7 9 10 8

MAD LIBS is a registered trademark of Penguin Random House LLC.

MAD LIBS®

GAME OVER! MAD LIBS

by Brandon T. Snider

Mad Libs
An Imprint of Penguin Random House

MAD LIBS

INSTRUCTIONS

MAD LIBS® is a game for people who don't like games! It can be played by one, two, three, four, or forty.

• RIDICULOUSLY SIMPLE DIRECTIONS

In this tablet you will find stories containing blank spaces where words are left out. One player, the READER, selects one of these stories. The READER does not tell anyone what the story is about. Instead, he/she asks the other players, the WRITERS, to give him/her words. These words are used to fill in the blank spaces in the story.

• TO PLAY

The READER asks each WRITER in turn to call out a word—an adjective or a noun or whatever the space calls for—and uses them to fill in the blank spaces in the story. The result is a MAD LIBS® game.

When the READER then reads the completed MAD LIBS® game to the other players, they will discover that they have written a story that is fantastic, screamingly funny, shocking, silly, crazy, or just plain dumb—depending upon which words each WRITER called out.

• EXAMPLE (Before and After)

"_____! " he said _____
    EXCLAMATION   ADVERB

as he jumped into his convertible _____ and
                                        NOUN

drove off with his _____ wife.
                       ADJECTIVE

"OUCH! " he said STUPIDLY
    EXCLAMATION   ADVERB

as he jumped into his convertible CAT and
                                        NOUN

drove off with his BRAVE wife.
                       ADJECTIVE

MAD LIBS®

QUICK REVIEW

In case you have forgotten what adjectives, adverbs, nouns, and verbs are, here is a quick review:

An ADJECTIVE describes something or somebody. *Lumpy, soft, ugly, messy,* and *short* are adjectives.

An ADVERB tells how something is done. It modifies a verb and usually ends in "ly." *Modestly, stupidly, greedily,* and *carefully* are adverbs.

A NOUN is the name of a person, place, or thing. *Sidewalk, umbrella, bridle, bathtub,* and *nose* are nouns.

A VERB is an action word. *Run, pitch, jump,* and *swim* are verbs. Put the verbs in past tense if the directions say PAST TENSE. *Ran, pitched, jumped,* and *swam* are verbs in the past tense.

When we ask for A PLACE, we mean any sort of place: a country or city *(Spain, Cleveland)* or a room *(bathroom, kitchen).*

An EXCLAMATION or SILLY WORD is any sort of funny sound, gasp, grunt, or outcry, like *Wow!, Ouch!, Whomp!, Ick!,* and *Gadzooks!*

When we ask for specific words, like a NUMBER, a COLOR, an ANIMAL, or a PART OF THE BODY, we mean a word that is one of those things, like *seven, blue, horse,* or *head.*

When we ask for a PLURAL, it means more than one. For example, *cat* pluralized is *cats.*

MAD LIBS® is fun to play with friends, but you can also play it by yourself! To begin with, DO NOT look at the story on the page below. Fill in the blanks on this page with the words called for. Then, using the words you have selected, fill in the blank spaces in the story.

Now you've created your own hilarious MAD LIBS® game!

PREPARE TO FIGHT!

ADJECTIVE _____

VERB ENDING IN "ING" _____

TYPE OF FOOD _____

NOUN _____

VERB _____

NUMBER _____

VERB _____

PART OF THE BODY (PLURAL) _____

VERB _____

TYPE OF FOOD _____

PLURAL NOUN _____

ADJECTIVE _____

ADJECTIVE _____

NOUN _____

NOUN _____

NOUN _____

VERB _____

Mario: What a/an _____ day, eh Luigi? The perfect day for
                              ADJECTIVE

_____ some Koopas. The _____ Kingdom is crawling
VERB ENDING IN "ING"   TYPE OF FOOD

with them!

Luigi: You're right about that, dear _____. I hope you're ready to
                                          NOUN

_____.
VERB

Mario: Ready? I've waited _____ years to _____ that scoundrel
                              NUMBER   VERB

Bowser!

Luigi: Pipe down. He has _____ everywhere.
                             PART OF THE BODY (PLURAL)

Mario: First, I'll _____ and grab a/an _____. That'll give me
                       VERB   TYPE OF FOOD

_____.
PLURAL NOUN

Luigi: And I'll grab a/an _____ star. Then I'll be the most _____
                             ADJECTIVE   ADJECTIVE

plumber of all time.

Mario: Remember we're there to rescue Princess _____, Luigi. Once we
                                                   NOUN

do that we'll be heroes!

Luigi: Then let's slide down that pipe and save the _____!
                                                        NOUN

Mario: That's the spirit, brother! Get your _____ ready. It's time to
                                                NOUN

_____!
VERB

MAD LIBS® is fun to play with friends, but you can also play it by yourself! To begin with, DO NOT look at the story on the page below. Fill in the blanks on this page with the words called for. Then, using the words you have selected, fill in the blank spaces in the story.

Now you've created your own hilarious MAD LIBS® game!

A LEGEND

NUMBER _____

ADJECTIVE _____

NOUN _____

COLOR _____

NOUN _____

VERB ENDING IN "ING" _____

ADJECTIVE _____

NOUN _____

ADJECTIVE _____

ADJECTIVE _____

FIRST NAME (FEMALE) _____

NOUN _____

ADJECTIVE _____

PLURAL NOUN _____

VERB _____

ADJECTIVE _____

PLURAL NOUN _____

VERB _____

MAD LIBS

A LEGEND

Hidden within the Kingdom of Hyrule are _____ pieces of a/an

NUMBER

_____ _____ known as the Triforce. This _____

ADJECTIVE   NOUN   COLOR

_____ holds the key to defeating the evil warlord Ganon and

NOUN

_____ Princess Zelda. Only the heroic Link can save the day!

VERB ENDING IN "ING"

He must use his _____ _____ to defeat _____

            ADJECTIVE   NOUN   ADJECTIVE

monsters and battle dark forces throughout the kingdom. Link will have to

fight his way through the _____ Woods, Lake _____ and

                   ADJECTIVE   FIRST NAME (FEMALE)

the famous Death _____! But first he'll need to find the _____

                NOUN   ADJECTIVE

Sword. Join Link as he collects _____ that will help him

                         PLURAL NOUN

_____ his enemies. Help him as he discovers _____ dungeons

VERB   ADJECTIVE

and explores lost _____. Will he be able to _____ the

           PLURAL NOUN   VERB

Princess in time? You decide!

GAMER GEAR MUST-HAVES!

ADJECTIVE _____

NOUN _____

A PLACE _____

ANIMAL _____

NUMBER _____

PLURAL NOUN _____

ADJECTIVE _____

NOUN _____

VERB _____

A PLACE _____

TYPE OF LIQUID _____

NOUN _____

VERB _____

ADJECTIVE _____

VERB ENDING IN "ING" _____

NUMBER _____

NOUN _____

MAD LIBS® is fun to play with friends, but you can also play it by yourself! To begin with, DO NOT look at the story on the page below. Fill in the blanks on this page with the words called for. Then, using the words you have selected, fill in the blank spaces in the story.

Now you've created your own hilarious MAD LIBS® game!

What does a gamer need in order to ensure ultimate victory?

- **Sound 'Splosion:** This _____ headset brings the
ADJECTIVE

   _____ straight to your _____! With sound so clear,
   NOUN   A PLACE

   you'll feel like a/an _____ tracking its prey.
                         ANIMAL

- **Crunch Trough:** After a long day of battling evil, you definitely

   need some snacks. How about _____ different
                                NUMBER

   varieties including Potato _____, Choco Bites, and
                              PLURAL NOUN

   _____ Frosted Mini Biscuits. Yum!
   ADJECTIVE

- **Vermintech:** This cordless _____ allows you to _____
                                NOUN   VERB

   without any hassle. It's so good you can even use it in (the) _____.
                                                                 A PLACE

- **Doozie Coozie:** Are you tired of your _____ spilling
                                           TYPE OF LIQUID

   all over your _____? Your drink will never _____
                 NOUN   VERB

   again with this _____ holder.
                   ADJECTIVE

- **Isolator 5000:** The ultimate _____ console is here!
                                  VERB ENDING IN "ING"

   _____ games at your disposal! You won't want to leave your
   NUMBER

   _____-room ever again!
   NOUN

MAD LIBS® is fun to play with friends, but you can also play it by yourself! To begin with, DO NOT look at the story on the page below. Fill in the blanks on this page with the words called for. Then, using the words you have selected, fill in the blank spaces in the story.

Now you've created your own hilarious MAD LIBS® game!

BUILD A WORLD
FROM SCRATCH

_____ NOUN

_____ COLOR

_____ ADJECTIVE

_____ NOUN

_____ OCCUPATION

_____ VERB

_____ OCCUPATION

_____ PLURAL NOUN

_____ ADJECTIVE

_____ ADVERB

_____ PLURAL NOUN

_____ VERB

_____ ADVERB

_____ NUMBER

_____ ANIMAL (PLURAL)

_____ ADJECTIVE

_____ NOUN

_____ VERB

MAD LIBS®
BUILD A WORLD
FROM SCRATCH

Step 1: Welcome to Peepsylvania! Choose a/an _____ for your Peep.
                                                    NOUN

It can be anything you want. It can even be _____. Just make sure it
                                              COLOR

looks _____. Remember, a Peep is a regular _____ just like
        ADJECTIVE   NOUN

you and me.

Step 2: Log in and begin! Your Peep needs a job. Is it a/an _____?
                                                                 OCCUPATION

Does it _____ all day long? Or it could be a/an _____
          VERB   OCCUPATION

instead. Then it would collect _____, but only if they're
                                  PLURAL NOUN

_____. Choose _____!
  ADJECTIVE   ADVERB

Step 3: Now it's time to make the _____. If you _____
                                         PLURAL NOUN   VERB

them, make sure you do it _____. Once you've assembled _____
                             ADVERB   NUMBER

_____, you're ready to start. Good luck!
  ANIMAL (PLURAL)

Step 4: You've reached the _____ level. Now your Peep is a Royal
                                  ADJECTIVE

_____. This allows it to _____ over all the other Peeps in
  NOUN   VERB

Peepsylvania. Congratulations!

MAD LIBS® is fun to play with friends, but you can also play it by yourself! To begin with, DO NOT look at the story on the page below. Fill in the blanks on this page with the words called for. Then, using the words you have selected, fill in the blank spaces in the story.

Now you've created your own hilarious MAD LIBS® game!

WELCOME!

_____ ADJECTIVE

_____ PLURAL NOUN

_____ OCCUPATION (PLURAL)

_____ ADJECTIVE

_____ NOUN

_____ ADJECTIVE

_____ VERB

_____ VERB

_____ VERB

_____ NOUN

_____ PERSON IN ROOM

_____ A PLACE

_____ A PLACE

_____ CITY

_____ NUMBER

_____ VERB

_____ PART OF THE BODY

MAD LIBS®
WELCOME!

Welcome to Skylands, a/an _____ kingdom high above the
                              ADJECTIVE

_____. It's here where a group of _____ use their
PLURAL NOUN   OCCUPATION (PLURAL)

abilities to combat the _____ forces of Kaos, an evil _____.
                        ADJECTIVE   NOUN

The _____ Skylanders _____ against Kaos using the power
    ADJECTIVE   VERB

of the Elements. Blast Zone can _____ with the power of Fire, and
                                VERB

Wash Buckler can _____ with the power of Water. For centuries, the
                 VERB

Skylanders protected the _____ of Light with the help of their mentors,
                         NOUN

the Portal Masters. One such mentor, known as _____, gathered
                                              PERSON IN ROOM

heroes from (the) _____, (the) _____, and _____.
                  A PLACE   A PLACE   CITY

Soon there were over _____ Skylanders ready to join the battle. Together
                     NUMBER

they _____ for what's right, even in the _____ of danger.
     VERB   PART OF THE BODY

MAD LIBS® is fun to play with friends, but you can also play it by yourself! To begin with, DO NOT look at the story on the page below. Fill in the blanks on this page with the words called for. Then, using the words you have selected, fill in the blank spaces in the story.

Now you've created your own hilarious MAD LIBS® game!

AN INSANE ASYLUM

_____ ADJECTIVE

_____ TYPE OF FOOD

_____ ADJECTIVE

_____ ADJECTIVE

_____ VERB

_____ ARTICLE OF CLOTHING

_____ ADJECTIVE

_____ NUMBER

_____ PLURAL NOUN

_____ NOUN

_____ VERB

_____ NOUN

_____ VERB

_____ ADJECTIVE

_____ A PLACE

_____ VERB

_____ VERB

Arkham Asylum is a/an _____ place. It's covered in darkness and
                         ADJECTIVE

smells like old _____. Is it the most _____ place in Gotham
                 TYPE OF FOOD   ADJECTIVE

City? Probably. And I'm trapped here with all the _____ inmates. My
                                                    ADJECTIVE

worst enemies have come together to _____ against me. It's a good
                                       VERB

thing I've got my utility _____. It's got everything I need
                           ARTICLE OF CLOTHING

including a/an _____ Laser, _____ _____, and
               ADJECTIVE   NUMBER   PLURAL NOUN

a/an _____ that can _____. I don't know if that will be
      NOUN   VERB

enough to stop the Clown _____ of Crime. The Joker continues to
                          NOUN

_____ Gotham with his _____ capers. Now he's taken control
  VERB   ADJECTIVE

of Arkham's _____ and wants to _____ it up. I've got to take
             A PLACE   VERB

him out in order to _____ the city. I'll show him what justice is all
                     VERB

about. No one can hide from Batman!

MAD LIBS® is fun to play with friends, but you can also play it by yourself! To begin with, DO NOT look at the story on the page below. Fill in the blanks on this page with the words called for. Then, using the words you have selected, fill in the blank spaces in the story.

Now you've created your own hilarious MAD LIBS® game!

PEPPERMINT CRUSH

FIRST NAME (FEMALE) _____

NOUN _____

ADJECTIVE _____

VERB ENDING IN "ING" _____

PERSON IN ROOM _____

VERB ENDING IN "ING" _____

NUMBER _____

A PLACE _____

ADJECTIVE _____

PLURAL NOUN _____

COLOR _____

VERB _____

COLOR _____

VERB ENDING IN "ING" _____

OCCUPATION _____

ADJECTIVE _____

NOUN _____

TYPE OF FOOD (PLURAL) _____

MAD LIBS®
PEPPERMINT CRUSH

Mom: _____, can you show me how to play *Peppermint Crush*? I
     FIRST NAME (FEMALE)

just downloaded it onto my new _____. It looks _____. So
                          NOUN   ADJECTIVE

many colors. How fun!

Daughter: Mom, I can't right now. I'm busy _____. Can't you
                                        VERB ENDING IN "ING"

ask _____?
  PERSON IN ROOM

Mom: I'm not _____ too much here. It'll only take _____
         VERB ENDING IN "ING"   NUMBER

minutes. Please? It will give me something to do when I'm at (the) _____.
                                                           A PLACE

Daughter: Fine! Whatever. It's _____. You just move the
                                ADJECTIVE

_____ together. They have to be the same color.
  PLURAL NOUN

Mom: What about the _____ ones? Can I _____ those with
                   COLOR   VERB

the _____ ones?
    COLOR

Daughter: No! Are you even _____?
                            VERB ENDING IN "ING"

Mom: Do not yell at me, please. I'm not a/an _____, and I'm not
                                       OCCUPATION

some _____ _____. I am your mother. Now help me collect
     ADJECTIVE   NOUN

more _____. I love you.
    TYPE OF FOOD (PLURAL)

MAD LIBS® is fun to play with friends, but you can also play it by yourself! To begin with, DO NOT look at the story on the page below. Fill in the blanks on this page with the words called for. Then, using the words you have selected, fill in the blank spaces in the story.

Now you've created your own hilarious MAD LIBS® game!

ONE MORE GAME

NOUN _____

ADJECTIVE _____

ADJECTIVE _____

PART OF THE BODY _____

VERB _____

A PLACE _____

CELEBRITY _____

ANIMAL _____

NUMBER _____

ADJECTIVE _____

LAST NAME _____

NOUN _____

TYPE OF FOOD _____

PERSON IN ROOM _____

FIRST NAME (MALE) _____

VERB ENDING IN "ING" _____

EXCLAMATION _____

VERB _____

MAD LIBS
ONE MORE GAME

Convincing your _____ to let you stay up past your bedtime to play
                     NOUN

video games can be _____, but it's not impossible. Here are some
                      ADJECTIVE

_____ excuses to use when you need one last game.
   ADJECTIVE

• My _____ hurts. The only way it'll feel better is if I
      PART OF THE BODY

_____ these cyborgs and save (the) _____.
   VERB   A PLACE

• _____ also plays _____ Hut so if you want me
     CELEBRITY   ANIMAL

to be successful in life, please give me _____ minutes to finish
                                            NUMBER

the _____ level.
     ADJECTIVE

• Mrs. _____, my _____ teacher, said that video games
        LAST NAME   NOUN

make you smart. She plays _____ *Assault*, so she knows.
                            TYPE OF FOOD

• There's nothing else to do! _____ isn't here to play with,
                               PERSON IN ROOM

Grandpa _____ went to bed, and it's _____
         FIRST NAME (MALE)   VERB ENDING IN "ING"

outside.

• _____! If you let me play *Night* _____, I'll
    EXCLAMATION   VERB

clean my room. Think about it.

MAD LIBS® is fun to play with friends, but you can also play it by yourself! To begin with, DO NOT look at the story on the page below. Fill in the blanks on this page with the words called for. Then, using the words you have selected, fill in the blank spaces in the story.

Now you've created your own hilarious MAD LIBS® game!

USE YOUR BRAIN

NOUN _____

ADJECTIVE _____

ANIMAL _____

ADJECTIVE _____

VERB _____

PART OF THE BODY _____

VERB ENDING IN "ING" _____

CITY _____

NOUN _____

NOUN _____

NUMBER _____

PLURAL NOUN _____

CELEBRITY _____

ADJECTIVE _____

PLURAL NOUN _____

TYPE OF FOOD (PLURAL) _____

NOUN _____

MAD LIBS®
USE YOUR BRAIN

A/An _____ is a terrible thing to waste. These games will keep your
      NOUN

brain _____!
   ADJECTIVE

Poke the Pig: This little _____ may not look _____, but looks
          ANIMAL   ADJECTIVE

can be deceiving. See if you can _____ it on its _____ as
              VERB   PART OF THE BODY

many times as possible. Remember, time is _____ out!
                       VERB ENDING IN "ING"

Trash Can City: Welcome to _____, the dirtiest place around. It's
              CITY

your job to pick up every _____ and put it in the _____
             NOUN   NOUN

before time runs out. You have _____ minutes to complete the task.
              NUMBER

Watch out for _____ that stand in your way.
      PLURAL NOUN

Meals For Math: Are you the _____ of the math world? You'll need
            CELEBRITY

to be in order to complete this _____ challenge. Collect a variety of
             ADJECTIVE

_____ and _____ and count them all up before
PLURAL NOUN   TYPE OF FOOD (PLURAL)

the _____ rings.
    NOUN

MAD LIBS® is fun to play with friends, but you can also play it by yourself! To begin with, DO NOT look at the story on the page below. Fill in the blanks on this page with the words called for. Then, using the words you have selected, fill in the blank spaces in the story.

Now you've created your own hilarious MAD LIBS® game!

WELCOME TO
THE FUTURE

NUMBER _____

ADJECTIVE _____

A PLACE _____

ADJECTIVE _____

ANIMAL (PLURAL) _____

ADJECTIVE _____

PLURAL NOUN _____

VERB _____

NOUN _____

A PLACE _____

PERSON IN ROOM _____

TYPE OF FOOD _____

PLURAL NOUN _____

A PLACE _____

ANIMAL _____

VERB _____

PLURAL NOUN _____

It's the year _____ and life is hard. A group of _____ robots
_____NUMBER_____ADJECTIVE

have taken control of (the) _____. They're using their magic weapons
A PLACE

to turn _____ human beings into _____. Things are bad.
ADJECTIVE ANIMAL (PLURAL)

There are _____ _____ oozing out of the streets. It isn't
ADJECTIVE PLURAL NOUN

safe anymore. You used to be able to _____ outside, but not anymore.
VERB

A/An _____ could see you and throw you in the _____ jail. I
NOUN A PLACE

spoke to _____ about getting more _____. The stash that
PERSON IN ROOM TYPE OF FOOD

we have tastes like rotten _____. We're hiding out in (the)
PLURAL NOUN

_____ now, but who knows what will happen next? A group of angry
A PLACE

_____-Men could strike at any time. Maybe we should _____
ANIMAL VERB

once and for all. Maybe it's time to raise our _____ in the air and
PLURAL NOUN

fight for what's right. That's what heroes would do.

MAD LIBS® is fun to play with friends, but you can also play it by yourself! To begin with, DO NOT look at the story on the page below. Fill in the blanks on this page with the words called for. Then, using the words you have selected, fill in the blank spaces in the story.

Now you've created your own hilarious MAD LIBS® game!

SMASH IT!

_____ VERB ENDING IN "ING"

_____ ANIMAL

_____ COLOR

_____ NOUN

_____ ADJECTIVE

_____ PLURAL NOUN

_____ ADJECTIVE

_____ COLOR

_____ VERB

_____ ADJECTIVE

_____ ANIMAL

_____ ANIMAL

_____ VERB ENDING IN "ING"

_____ VERB

_____ ADVERB

_____ VERB

_____ ADVERB

It's time for a battle royal. Who's _____ today?
VERB ENDING IN "ING"
Let's see what these brawlers can do.

Pikachu is a Pokémon that resembles a/an _____ and can shoot bolts of
ANIMAL
electricity from the _____ dots on his cheeks. Protecting his
COLOR
_____ is not one of his strong suits.
NOUN

Wario can be _____ and gross during battle. He's been
ADJECTIVE
known to produce stinky _____ during a fight. Beware of
PLURAL NOUN
his _____ strength and his love of _____ coins.
ADJECTIVE COLOR

Snake can _____ very well and is a/an _____ tactician. He's
VERB ADJECTIVE
also quick like a/an _____ .
ANIMAL

Duck Hunt combines the mischievousness of a/an _____ with the
ANIMAL
_____ skills of a duck. Together they _____ their
VERB ENDING IN "ING" VERB
enemies _____ .
ADVERB

Pac-Man is superfast and can _____ _____ . And he does it
VERB ADVERB
all with a smile.

MAD LIBS® is fun to play with friends, but you can also play it by yourself! To begin with, DO NOT look at the story on the page below. Fill in the blanks on this page with the words called for. Then, using the words you have selected, fill in the blank spaces in the story.

Now you've created your own hilarious MAD LIBS® game!

BATTLE BUDS

NOUN _____

VERB _____

ADJECTIVE _____

NOUN _____

NOUN _____

ANIMAL (PLURAL) _____

NOUN _____

ADJECTIVE _____

ADJECTIVE _____

NOUN _____

NOUN _____

ADJECTIVE _____

NOUN _____

NUMBER _____

PERSON IN ROOM _____

TYPE OF FOOD _____

TYPE OF LIQUID _____

Welcome to mindscape. Players, are you ready?

Kevin: Dude, are you ready for me to destroy your _____?

NOUN

Colin: Ha-ha. You can't _____ anything with that _____

VERB   ADJECTIVE

_____ of yours. It can barely function. You need a real _____.

NOUN   NOUN

Then you'll be able to use maximum power.

Kevin: Look out! A group of _____ are right behind you. Blast them

ANIMAL (PLURAL)

with your _____!

NOUN

Colin: That's too _____. I need something a little more _____

ADJECTIVE   ADJECTIVE

like a/an _____.

NOUN

Kevin: Whatever. Did you do your _____ homework? It was pretty

NOUN

_____.

ADJECTIVE

Colin: Not yet. Hey, can I buy a magic _____ from you? I've got

NOUN

_____ credits.

NUMBER

Kevin: Hold on. _____ is calling me. I think its dinnertime. We're

PERSON IN ROOM

having _____.

TYPE OF FOOD

Colin: That's cool. I just spilled _____ all over my keyboard

TYPE OF LIQUID

anyway. Till next time, buddy!

MAD LIBS® is fun to play with friends, but you can also play it by yourself! To begin with, DO NOT look at the story on the page below. Fill in the blanks on this page with the words called for. Then, using the words you have selected, fill in the blank spaces in the story.

Now you've created your own hilarious MAD LIBS® game!

MEGA QUIZ

OCCUPATION _____

NOUN _____

VERB ENDING IN "ING" _____

ANIMAL _____

VERB _____

ADJECTIVE _____

OCCUPATION _____

NOUN _____

ADJECTIVE _____

NOUN _____

VERB ENDING IN "ING" _____

MAD LIBS®
MEGA QUIZ

How well do you know Mega Man and his villains? Take this quiz and see!

1. Who is the brilliant _____ who uses his evil _____ to create
   OCCUPATION   NOUN

   robots bent on _____ Mega Man?
                  VERB ENDING IN "ING"

   A.   Professor Evil   C.   Dr. Wily

   B.   Wicked Willy   D.   Professor Man

2. Who uses his search _____ to _____ up walls?
                        ANIMAL   VERB

   A.   Slither   C.   The Fox

   B.   Snake Man   D.   Birdman

3. This villain is a/an _____ _____ who uses a sharp
                         ADJECTIVE   OCCUPATION

   _____ to pierce _____ surfaces.
       NOUN   ADJECTIVE

   A.   Tomahawk Man   C.   Clown Man

   B.   Splash Woman   D.   Zebular

4. This bad guy has a/an _____ on his head and loves
                            NOUN

   _____. He's a bit of a daredevil.
   VERB ENDING IN "ING"

   A.   Star Man   C.   Bomb Man

   B.   Wily Capsule   D.   Stone Man

MAD LIBS® is fun to play with friends, but you can also play it by yourself! To begin with, DO NOT look at the story on the page below. Fill in the blanks on this page with the words called for. Then, using the words you have selected, fill in the blank spaces in the story.

Now you've created your own hilarious MAD LIBS® game!

LET'S DRIVE: MYRTLE BEACH

—————————————————— ADJECTIVE

—————————————————— PLURAL NOUN

—————————————————— PLURAL NOUN

—————————————————— ADJECTIVE

—————————————————— VEHICLE

—————————————————— TYPE OF FOOD

—————————————————— ANIMAL (PLURAL)

—————————————————— PART OF THE BODY (PLURAL)

—————————————————— NOUN

—————————————————— SILLY WORD

—————————————————— NOUN

—————————————————— NOUN

—————————————————— VERB

—————————————————— NOUN

—————————————————— ADJECTIVE

MAD☺LIBS®
LET'S DRIVE: MYRTLE BEACH

Welcome to the Grand Strand—where the people are hot and the cars are

_____ .
   ADJECTIVE

But _____ can be deceiving. There's sun, _____, and a/an
   PLURAL NOUN   PLURAL NOUN

_____ ocean, but that doesn't mean crime takes a vacation. Gas up
   ADJECTIVE

your _____ and head down to the boulevard for some _____ .
   VEHICLE   TYPE OF FOOD

But be careful, there are _____ everywhere waiting to strike. Take a
               ANIMAL (PLURAL)

good look around. Use your _____ . It's up to you to figure
                 PART OF THE BODY (PLURAL)

out who's a friend and who's a/an _____ . Once you meet Doctor
                          NOUN

_____ , he'll tell you where to find the _____ . Just remember,
   SILLY WORD   NOUN

don't trust anyone, not even your own _____ . People are waiting to
                         NOUN

_____ you all over this city. Some people say life's a/an _____ .
   VERB   NOUN

Well, they've never been to _____ Beach.
                ADJECTIVE

MAD LIBS® is fun to play with friends, but you can also play it by yourself! To begin with, DO NOT look at the story on the page below. Fill in the blanks on this page with the words called for. Then, using the words you have selected, fill in the blank spaces in the story.

Now you've created your own hilarious MAD LIBS® game!

WORK IT OUT

VERB ENDING IN "ING" _____

VERB _____

PART OF THE BODY _____

ADJECTIVE _____

NUMBER _____

NOUN _____

ADJECTIVE _____

PART OF THE BODY _____

VERB _____

NOUN _____

PART OF THE BODY _____

VERB _____

ANIMAL _____

ADJECTIVE _____

VERB _____

NUMBER _____

PART OF THE BODY _____

NOUN _____

MAD LIBS
WORK IT OUT

There's no _____ in *Workout World*. There's only working out!
<small>VERB ENDING IN "ING"</small>

Set your controls to fun and get ready to _____.
<small>VERB</small>

Wind grasp: Use your _____ to grab as much wind as
<small>PART OF THE BODY</small>

possible and put it into your _____ pouch. Once you have _____
<small>ADJECTIVE</small> <small>NUMBER</small>

pouches filled, dump them out and start over.

Exercise penny: Bend down and place a/an _____ on the ground in
<small>NOUN</small>

front of you. Stare at it until you feel _____. Repeat as needed.
<small>ADJECTIVE</small>

Wiggle worm: Take your _____ and _____ it like it's a hot
<small>PART OF THE BODY</small> <small>VERB</small>

_____. Then take your other _____ and _____
<small>NOUN</small> <small>PART OF THE BODY</small> <small>VERB</small>

it like it's a/an _____. Congratulations. You're a wiggle worm.
<small>ANIMAL</small>

Sittin' mat: Get out your _____ mat and _____ on it for
<small>ADJECTIVE</small> <small>VERB</small>

_____ minutes. This will allow your _____ to relax. Feel the
<small>NUMBER</small> <small>PART OF THE BODY</small>

_____ move through you.
<small>NOUN</small>

MAD LIBS® is fun to play with friends, but you can also play it by yourself! To begin with, DO NOT look at the story on the page below. Fill in the blanks on this page with the words called for. Then, using the words you have selected, fill in the blank spaces in the story.

Now you've created your own hilarious MAD LIBS® game!

ZOMBIE INVASION

SILLY WORD _____

NOUN _____

NOUN _____

ADJECTIVE _____

ADJECTIVE _____

PLURAL NOUN _____

TYPE OF FOOD (PLURAL) _____

VERB _____

ANIMAL _____

CELEBRITY (MALE) _____

EXCLAMATION _____

PLURAL NOUN _____

ADJECTIVE _____

SILLY WORD _____

NOUN _____

A PLACE _____

NOUN _____

FIRST NAME (MALE) _____

MAD LIBS®
ZOMBIE INVASION

Dear Aunt _____,
SILLY WORD

I hope this _____ gets to you. I might be the last person on Planet
NOUN

_____ . It's really _____ here because of all the zombies. They
NOUN   ADJECTIVE

aren't like the _____ zombies we used to watch on TV. They actually
ADJECTIVE

eat _____ and _____! I saw one of them
PLURAL NOUN   TYPE OF FOOD (PLURAL)

_____ a/an _____ the other day. It was more mean than
VERB   ANIMAL

scary. Sometimes I think, "What would _____ do in my situation?"
CELEBRITY (MALE)

I think he would say, "_____! It's time to get out our
EXCLAMATION

_____ and save the world!" Anyway, I hope this letter isn't too
PLURAL NOUN

_____ . Please tell Uncle _____ that I say hello. Are you going
ADJECTIVE   SILLY WORD

anywhere this _____? I'd go to (the) _____, but I think there
NOUN   A PLACE

might be too many zombies there. Have a good _____!
NOUN

Love,

_____
FIRST NAME (MALE)

MAD LIBS® is fun to play with friends, but you can also play it by yourself! To begin with, DO NOT look at the story on the page below. Fill in the blanks on this page with the words called for. Then, using the words you have selected, fill in the blank spaces in the story.

Now you've created your own hilarious MAD LIBS® game!

LET'S FIGHT!

_____ NOUN

_____ PART OF THE BODY (PLURAL)

_____ VERB

_____ ADJECTIVE

_____ OCCUPATION

_____ VERB ENDING IN "ING"

_____ VERB

_____ PLURAL NOUN

_____ PLURAL NOUN

_____ PART OF THE BODY (PLURAL)

_____ ANIMAL

_____ ADJECTIVE

_____ SILLY WORD

_____ ADJECTIVE

_____ A PLACE

_____ TYPE OF FOOD

_____ VERB ENDING IN "ING"

_____ PART OF THE BODY (PLURAL)

MAD LIBS®
LET'S FIGHT!

They're the best at what they do, and what they do is fight! They are the

awesome stars of _____ *Fighter*.
                    NOUN

Ryu: He may not use his _____ very much, but his fists
                              PART OF THE BODY (PLURAL)

_____ for him. Ryu is a/an _____ student who is serious
   VERB   ADJECTIVE

about becoming a master _____. He's always _____
                          OCCUPATION   VERB ENDING IN "ING"

his enemy, waiting for the right time to _____.
                                            VERB

Cammy: Cammy keeps her _____ close and her _____
                            PLURAL NOUN   PLURAL NOUN

closer. Don't let her kind _____ fool you—she also goes by
                           PART OF THE BODY (PLURAL)

the nickname Killer _____.
                      ANIMAL

Bison: There is no one more _____ than Bison. He craves power. A
                                ADJECTIVE

country like _____ will never be enough for him. He won't stop until
             SILLY WORD

he's the most _____ martial artist in the entire _____.
               ADJECTIVE   A PLACE

Chun-Li: When it comes to superfast reflexes, Chun-Li takes the _____.
                                                                    TYPE OF FOOD

Her kick sends her enemies _____ to the ground on their
                           VERB ENDING IN "ING"

_____.
PART OF THE BODY (PLURAL)

GOOD-BYE FOREVER

_____ FIRST NAME

_____ A PLACE

_____ ADJECTIVE

_____ PERSON IN ROOM

_____ TYPE OF FOOD

_____ NOUN

_____ ADJECTIVE

_____ ANIMAL

_____ ADJECTIVE

_____ PLURAL NOUN

_____ PART OF THE BODY (PLURAL)

_____ PERSON IN ROOM

_____ A PLACE

_____ CELEBRITY

_____ PLURAL NOUN

_____ FIRST NAME

MAD LIBS® is fun to play with friends, but you can also play it by yourself! To begin with, DO NOT look at the story on the page below. Fill in the blanks on this page with the words called for. Then, using the words you have selected, fill in the blank spaces in the story.

Now you've created your own hilarious MAD LIBS® game!

MAD LIBS
GOOD-BYE FOREVER

Dear _____,
       FIRST NAME

I'm sorry to tell you this, but I'm leaving you. Every day I come home from

(the) _____ and you're playing _____ *Fortress* with
        A PLACE   ADJECTIVE

_____. What about our time together? You said you would take me
PERSON IN ROOM

out for _____ on _____ Day, but you never did. You said you
         TYPE OF FOOD   NOUN

would take me to see *The* _____ _____ *of Mr. Marlow,* but
                            ADJECTIVE   ANIMAL

you never did. It's my _____ movie! All you want to do is shoot
                        ADJECTIVE

_____ at people's _____ on the computer. It's
PLURAL NOUN   PART OF THE BODY (PLURAL)

ruining my life. Even _____ said that you play too much! When are
                      PERSON IN ROOM

we going to (the) _____? When are you introducing me to _____?
                   A PLACE   CELEBRITY

I guess those were all lies. Thanks for the _____ but it's over. Good-
                                             PLURAL NOUN

bye forever.

Sincerely,

_____
FIRST NAME

MAD LIBS® is fun to play with friends, but you can also play it by yourself! To begin with, DO NOT look at the story on the page below. Fill in the blanks on this page with the words called for. Then, using the words you have selected, fill in the blank spaces in the story.

Now you've created your own hilarious MAD LIBS® game!

ROBOT VAMPIRE NINJA PIRATE & FRIENDS

_____ NOUN

_____ ANIMAL (PLURAL)

_____ NOUN

_____ ADJECTIVE

_____ A PLACE

_____ TYPE OF LIQUID

_____ NOUN

_____ NOUN

_____ TYPE OF FOOD

_____ NOUN

_____ ADJECTIVE

_____ ADJECTIVE

_____ VERB

_____ PERSON IN ROOM

_____ ADJECTIVE

MAD LIBS®
ROBOT VAMPIRE
NINJA PIRATE & FRIENDS

Are you looking for a/an _____ that gives you action, excitement, and

NOUN

an army of cloned _____? Look no further! This game has everything.

ANIMAL (PLURAL)

A wicked _____ Queen cast a/an _____ spell that turned

NOUN   ADJECTIVE

everyone in (the) _____ into _____. Now it's up to Robot

A PLACE   TYPE OF LIQUID

Vampire Ninja Pirate and his friends to save the _____. It won't be

NOUN

easy though. This isn't _____-ball. It's a good thing they brought

NOUN

_____, because they're going to need it. Will _____ Man and

TYPE OF FOOD   NOUN

_____ Lady use their powers to reverse the spell? Or maybe Robot

ADJECTIVE

Vampire Ninja Pirate will use his _____ blaster to _____ the

ADJECTIVE   VERB

Queen and end her reign of terror? It's all up to _____. Log on today

PERSON IN ROOM

for your free _____ codes and join the battle!

ADJECTIVE

MAD LIBS® is fun to play with friends, but you can also play it by yourself! To begin with, DO NOT look at the story on the page below. Fill in the blanks on this page with the words called for. Then, using the words you have selected, fill in the blank spaces in the story.

Now you've created your own hilarious MAD LIBS® game!

THE EXCELLENT
ANTONIO TRIPLETS

VEHICLE _____

ADJECTIVE _____

A PLACE _____

VERB _____

PLURAL NOUN _____

PART OF THE BODY (PLURAL) _____

VERB _____

ADJECTIVE _____

PART OF THE BODY (PLURAL) _____

NOUN _____

ADJECTIVE _____

ANIMAL _____

TYPE OF LIQUID _____

NOUN _____

VERB ENDING IN "ING" _____

ADJECTIVE _____

ADJECTIVE _____

OCCUPATION _____

MAD LIBS®
THE EXCELLENT
ANTONIO TRIPLETS

Alfonso: Prince Grape has been kidnapped! Time to hop in the _____

VEHICLE

and go to _____ City.

ADJECTIVE

Giovanni: No, Alfonso! We are electricians from (the) _____. We are

A PLACE

not some kind of heroes.

Sal: We are triplets who _____ when duty calls! If the Brussels Sprout

VERB

Kingdom needs us then we will strap _____ on our

PLURAL NOUN

_____ and do the job.

PART OF THE BODY (PLURAL)

Giovanni: But the Salamander Queen can _____! She has

VERB

_____ _____. What can we do? Throw a/an

ADJECTIVE · PART OF THE BODY (PLURAL)

_____ at her?

NOUN

Alfonso: Brother, we must be like the _____ _____. We'll

ADJECTIVE · ANIMAL

sneak up on her with our _____ guns and then, when she is resting

TYPE OF LIQUID

on her _____, we will strike!

NOUN

Sal: Personally, I look forward to _____ her _____

VERB ENDING IN "ING" · ADJECTIVE

minions. Let us do it for Prince Grape.

Giovanni: You both make very _____ points. It's time to be a/an

ADJECTIVE

_____. For Prince Grape!

OCCUPATION

MAD LIBS® is fun to play with friends, but you can also play it by yourself! To begin with, DO NOT look at the story on the page below. Fill in the blanks on this page with the words called for. Then, using the words you have selected, fill in the blank spaces in the story.

Now you've created your own hilarious MAD LIBS® game!

CONVENTION TIME!

NOUN _____

ADJECTIVE _____

NOUN _____

TYPE OF FOOD (PLURAL) _____

NUMBER _____

PERSON IN ROOM _____

NOUN _____

A PLACE _____

ARTICLE OF CLOTHING _____

NOUN _____

VERB _____

ADJECTIVE _____

NOUN _____

PERSON IN ROOM _____

PLURAL NOUN _____

NOUN _____

MAD LIBS®
CONVENTION TIME!

Welcome to Gamer Con 5000! We're excited to have you. Please

check your _____ for a list of _____ items you may bring
NOUN / ADJECTIVE

inside the _____. _____ are strictly prohibited!
NOUN / TYPE OF FOOD (PLURAL)

Gaming Centers will be set up in _____ locations, and attendees will be
NUMBER

divided up by character. If you are dressed as _____ from
PERSON IN ROOM

_____, please check in at (the) _____. If you are wearing
NOUN / A PLACE

a/an _____, you will be denied entry unless accompanied by
ARTICLE OF CLOTHING

your _____. Attendees looking to play *Star* _____ and *The*
NOUN / VERB

_____ _____ should register online. No one dressed as
ADJECTIVE / NOUN

_____ will be allowed in the bathrooms for any reason. Please bring
PERSON IN ROOM

extra _____ and remember to have a/an _____!
PLURAL NOUN / NOUN

MEOW LIBS

by Sarah Fabiny

Mad Libs
An Imprint of Penguin Random House

INSTRUCTIONS

MAD LIBS® is a game for people who don't like games!
It can be played by one, two, three, four, or forty.

• RIDICULOUSLY SIMPLE DIRECTIONS

In this tablet you will find stories containing blank spaces where words are left out.
One player, the READER, selects one of these stories. The READER does not tell anyone
what the story is about. Instead, he/she asks the other players, the WRITERS, to give
him/her words. These words are used to fill in the blank spaces in the story.

• TO PLAY

The READER asks each WRITER in turn to call out a word—an adjective or a noun or
whatever the space calls for—and uses them to fill in the blank spaces in the story. The
result is a MAD LIBS® game.

When the READER then reads the completed MAD LIBS® game to the other players,
they will discover that they have written a story that is fantastic, screamingly funny,
shocking, silly, crazy, or just plain dumb—depending upon which words each WRITER
called out.

• EXAMPLE (*Before* and *After*)

"_____!" he said _____
　　　　　EXCLAMATION　　　　　　　　　　　　　　　ADVERB

as he jumped into his convertible _____ and
　　　　　　　　　　　　　　　　　　　　　NOUN

drove off with his _____ wife.
　　　　　　　　　ADJECTIVE

"_____OUCH_____!" he said _____STUPIDLY_____
　　　　EXCLAMATION　　　　　　　　　　　　　ADVERB

as he jumped into his convertible _____CAT_____ and
　　　　　　　　　　　　　　　　　　　NOUN

drove off with his _____BRAVE_____ wife.
　　　　　　　　　ADJECTIVE

MAD LIBS®

QUICK REVIEW

In case you have forgotten what adjectives, adverbs, nouns, and verbs are, here is a quick review:

An ADJECTIVE describes something or somebody. *Lumpy, soft, ugly, messy,* and *short* are adjectives.

An ADVERB tells how something is done. It modifies a verb and usually ends in "ly." *Modestly, stupidly, greedily,* and *carefully* are adverbs.

A NOUN is the name of a person, place, or thing. *Sidewalk, umbrella, bridle, bathtub,* and *nose* are nouns.

A VERB is an action word. *Run, pitch, jump,* and *swim* are verbs. Put the verbs in past tense if the directions say PAST TENSE. *Ran, pitched, jumped,* and *swam* are verbs in the past tense.

When we ask for A PLACE, we mean any sort of place: a country or city *(Spain, Cleveland)* or a room *(bathroom, kitchen).*

An EXCLAMATION or SILLY WORD is any sort of funny sound, gasp, grunt, or outcry, like *Wow!, Ouch!, Whomp!, Ick!,* and *Gadzooks!*

When we ask for specific words, like a NUMBER, a COLOR, an ANIMAL, or a PART OF THE BODY, we mean a word that is one of those things, like *seven, blue, horse,* or *head.*

When we ask for a PLURAL, it means more than one. For example, *cat* pluralized is *cats.*

MAD LIBS® is fun to play with friends, but you can also play it by yourself! To begin with, DO NOT look at the story on the page below. Fill in the blanks on this page with the words called for. Then, using the words you have selected, fill in the blank spaces in the story.

Now you've created your own hilarious MAD LIBS® game!

FAMOUS CATS

ADJECTIVE _____

NOUN _____

NUMBER _____

TYPE OF FOOD _____

PLURAL NOUN _____

VERB _____

PERSON IN ROOM _____

PERSON IN ROOM (FEMALE) _____

PLURAL NOUN _____

NOUN _____

PART OF THE BODY _____

A PLACE _____

PERSON IN ROOM (FEMALE) _____

ADJECTIVE _____

ANIMAL _____

MAD LIBS
FAMOUS CATS

From cartoons to social media, cats are everywhere. Here are a few of the most

famous cats:

- Morris—the cat with the _____ attitude and the posh

ADJECTIVE

  _____ is the "spokesperson" for _____ Lives cat

NOUN — — — — — — — — — — — NUMBER

  _____.

TYPE OF FOOD

- Garfield—the famous comic-strip cat who hates _____, loves

PLURAL NOUN

  to _____, and has no respect for _____, his

VERB — — — — — — — — — PERSON IN ROOM

  owner's dog.

- Smelly Cat—made famous in the song sung by _____

PERSON IN ROOM (FEMALE)

  on the TV show _____.

PLURAL NOUN

- Grumpy Cat—an Internet _____ known for her hilarious

NOUN

  _____ expressions.

PART OF THE BODY

- Stubbs—the mayor of (the) _____, Alaska.

A PLACE

- Cat—the feline heroine of the movie *Breakfast at*

  _____'s.

PERSON IN ROOM (FEMALE)

- Tom—the _____ cat that will never catch his archenemy,

ADJECTIVE

  Jerry the _____.

ANIMAL

MAD LIBS® is fun to play with friends, but you can also play it by yourself! To begin with, DO NOT look at the story on the page below. Fill in the blanks on this page with the words called for. Then, using the words you have selected, fill in the blank spaces in the story.

Now you've created your own hilarious MAD LIBS® game!

WHICH BREED IS RIGHT FOR YOU?

———————————————— PART OF THE BODY (PLURAL)

———————————————— ADJECTIVE

———————————————— NOUN

———————————————— ADJECTIVE

———————————————— NOUN

———————————————— NOUN

———————————————— PART OF THE BODY (PLURAL)

———————————————— ADJECTIVE

———————————————— NOUN

———————————————— SILLY WORD

———————————————— ADJECTIVE

———————————————— A PLACE

———————————————— ADJECTIVE

———————————————— PART OF THE BODY

———————————————— COLOR

———————————————— ADJECTIVE

———————————————— NOUN

MAD LIBS®
WHICH BREED IS RIGHT FOR YOU?

So you're thinking of getting a cat. Whether you prefer cats with no

_____ or _____ ears, there's a/an _____
PART OF THE BODY (PLURAL)   ADJECTIVE   NOUN

for you.

Sphynx: If you go for the _____ things in life, and don't want to
                                ADJECTIVE

have to clean up cat hair, this is the _____ for you.
                                        NOUN

Siamese: Do you want a cat that sounds like a crying _____ and has
                                                          NOUN

crossed _____? Well then, go get a Siamese.
        PART OF THE BODY (PLURAL)

Manx: Looking for a cat with a sweet, _____ face and no
                                           ADJECTIVE

_____? We suggest you get a/an _____.
NOUN   SILLY WORD

Maine coon: How about a cat that's the size of a/an _____ dog? If
                                                         ADJECTIVE

you don't mind having to brush your cat every day, it sounds like you should

get a/an _____ coon.
          A PLACE

Persian: If you love a/an _____-looking cat with a scrunched-up
                               ADJECTIVE

_____, go get yourself a Persian.
PART OF THE BODY

Snowshoe: Do you love a cat with adorable _____ feet and a/an
                                               COLOR

_____ personality? You may want a/an _____-shoe.
ADJECTIVE   NOUN

MAD LIBS® is fun to play with friends, but you can also play it by yourself! To begin with, DO NOT look at the story on the page below. Fill in the blanks on this page with the words called for. Then, using the words you have selected, fill in the blank spaces in the story.

Now you've created your own hilarious MAD LIBS® game!

CAT SAYINGS

ADJECTIVE _____

PLURAL NOUN _____

PART OF THE BODY _____

NOUN _____

SILLY WORD _____

ADJECTIVE _____

VERB ENDING IN "ING" _____

ARTICLE OF CLOTHING _____

ADJECTIVE _____

NOUN _____

ANIMAL _____

NOUN _____

NOUN _____

EXCLAMATION _____

ADJECTIVE _____

ADVERB _____

ADJECTIVE _____

MAD LIBS
CAT SAYINGS

There are a lot of _____ phrases that incorporate our favorite feline
          ADJECTIVE

_____. Check out these sayings and their meanings:
PLURAL NOUN

- Cat got your _____?: Why aren't you talking?
          PART OF THE BODY

- You let the cat out of the _____: _____! My secret
          NOUN   SILLY WORD

    isn't so _____ anymore.
       ADJECTIVE

- It is raining cats and dogs: It is _____ like crazy.
          VERB ENDING IN "ING"

- That is the cat's _____: That is totally _____!
         ARTICLE OF CLOTHING   ADJECTIVE

- When the cat's away, the mice will play: The boss is away—let's get this

    _____ started!
     NOUN

- Curiosity killed the _____: Mind your own _____!
          ANIMAL   NOUN

- He is a fat cat: He likes to flash his _____.
         NOUN

- Looks like something the cat dragged in: _____! You look
          EXCLAMATION

    _____. What happened?!
    ADJECTIVE

- Cat on a hot tin roof: Please sit _____!
         ADVERB

- It's like herding cats: This job is totally _____!
         ADJECTIVE

MAD LIBS® is fun to play with friends, but you can also play it by yourself! To begin with, DO NOT look at the story on the page below. Fill in the blanks on this page with the words called for. Then, using the words you have selected, fill in the blank spaces in the story.

Now you've created your own hilarious MAD LIBS® game!

CAT SHOWS

_____ ADJECTIVE

_____ ADJECTIVE

_____ ADJECTIVE

_____ VERB

_____ NOUN

_____ SAME NOUN

_____ NOUN

_____ NOUN

_____ PLURAL NOUN

_____ PLURAL NOUN

_____ NOUN

_____ A PLACE

_____ PLURAL NOUN

_____ ADJECTIVE

_____ NOUN

There are some cat owners who take their love of cats to a/an _____
ADJECTIVE

level. A/An _____ example of this: the cat show. Both _____
ADJECTIVE   _ADJECTIVE_

and purebred cats are allowed to _____ in a cat show, although the
VERB

rules differ from _____ to _____. The cats are compared
NOUN   _SAME NOUN_

to a breed _____, and those judged to be closest to it are awarded
NOUN

a/an _____. At the end of the year, all the _____ who
NOUN   _PLURAL NOUN_

won at various shows are tallied up, and regional and national _____
PLURAL NOUN

are presented. The very first cat _____ took place in 1598 at (the)
NOUN

_____ in England. In the United States, the first cat shows were held
A PLACE

at New England country _____ in the 1860s. The most important
PLURAL NOUN

cat show in the United States is the CFA _____ Cat Show. But no
ADJECTIVE

matter which cat wins "Best in Show," every cat is a/an _____—to
NOUN

their owners, at least!

MAD LIBS® is fun to play with friends, but you can also play it by yourself! To begin with, DO NOT look at the story on the page below. Fill in the blanks on this page with the words called for. Then, using the words you have selected, fill in the blank spaces in the story.

Now you've created your own hilarious MAD LIBS® game!

CATS IN THE NEWS

PLURAL NOUN _____

ADJECTIVE _____

NOUN _____

ADJECTIVE _____

NUMBER _____

NOUN _____

NOUN _____

NOUN _____

SAME NOUN _____

ADJECTIVE _____

NOUN _____

ADJECTIVE _____

NOUN _____

VERB _____

MAD LIBS®
CATS IN THE NEWS

News Anchor #1: Stay tuned, _____! After the commercial break, we
PLURAL NOUN

have a/an _____ story about a cat who saved a young _____
ADJECTIVE   NOUN

from a/an _____ dog.
ADJECTIVE

News Anchor #2: That reminds me of the story about the cat that dialed

_____-1-1 after its owner fell out of his _____.
NUMBER   NOUN

News Anchor #1: And how about that kitten that survived the deadly

_____ in Taiwan?
NOUN

News Anchor #2: Have you heard about the kitten that was saved from a/an

_____ by a/an _____-fighter with _____ water
NOUN   SAME NOUN   ADJECTIVE

and a/an _____ full of oxygen?
NOUN

News Anchor #1: And who could forget that _____ story about a
ADJECTIVE

cat that took a/an _____ on the London Underground?
NOUN

News Anchor #2: Well, I guess he had to _____ to work just like
VERB

everyone else!

MAD LIBS® is fun to play with friends, but you can also play it by yourself! To begin with, DO NOT look at the story on the page below. Fill in the blanks on this page with the words called for. Then, using the words you have selected, fill in the blank spaces in the story.

Now you've created your own hilarious MAD LIBS® game!

HISTORY OF CATS

_____ VERB ENDING IN "ING"

_____ NUMBER

_____ ADJECTIVE

_____ ANIMAL (PLURAL)

_____ SAME ANIMAL (PLURAL)

_____ ADJECTIVE

_____ PLURAL NOUN

_____ ADJECTIVE

_____ PART OF THE BODY

_____ ADJECTIVE

_____ OCCUPATION (PLURAL)

_____ VERB (PAST TENSE)

_____ ADJECTIVE

_____ ADJECTIVE

_____ NUMBER

_____ ADJECTIVE

MAD LIBS®
HISTORY OF CATS

Cats have been _____ with—or at least tolerating—people for
                  VERB ENDING IN "ING"

over _____ years. Cats first became a part of our _____ lives
        NUMBER   ADJECTIVE

when people started to grow grain. The grain attracted _____,
                                                        ANIMAL (PLURAL)

and the cats preyed on the _____. Cats soon became
                            SAME ANIMAL (PLURAL)

a/an _____ fixture in peoples' _____ and were even
      ADJECTIVE   PLURAL NOUN

worshipped in _____ Egypt. There was even an Egyptian goddess
               ADJECTIVE

that had the _____ of a cat! However, in the _____
             PART OF THE BODY   ADJECTIVE

Ages, cats came to be demonized and were thought to be affiliated with evil

_____. Many cats were _____ to ward off evil. In
OCCUPATION (PLURAL)   VERB (PAST TENSE)

the 1600s, the cat's _____ reputation was restored, and today cats
                     ADJECTIVE

are _____ stars and live in _____ percent of American
     ADJECTIVE   NUMBER

households. Talk about a long and _____ history!
                                   ADJECTIVE

MAD LIBS® is fun to play with friends, but you can also play it by yourself! To begin with, DO NOT look at the story on the page below. Fill in the blanks on this page with the words called for. Then, using the words you have selected, fill in the blank spaces in the story.

Now you've created your own hilarious MAD LIBS® game!

I AM A CAT LADY

ADJECTIVE _____

ADJECTIVE _____

PLURAL NOUN _____

NUMBER _____

ADJECTIVE _____

ADJECTIVE _____

VERB _____

ADJECTIVE _____

PLURAL NOUN _____

ADVERB _____

ADVERB _____

NOUN _____

ADJECTIVE _____

ADJECTIVE _____

ADJECTIVE _____

ANIMAL _____

MAD☺LIBS®
I AM A CAT LADY

Dear _____ Neighbor,
　　　　　ADJECTIVE

I'm glad we have come to a/an _____ understanding about our
　　　　　　　　　　　　　　　　　ADJECTIVE

_____ . You have come to accept my _____ cats, and
PLURAL NOUN　　　　　　　　　　　　　　　　　NUMBER

I have come to accept your _____ dog. Yes, my _____
　　　　　　　　　　　　　ADJECTIVE　　　　　　　　　　　ADJECTIVE

cats may _____ in your garden, but your _____ dog
　　　　　VERB　　　　　　　　　　　　　　　　　ADJECTIVE

digs up my _____ . And I will remind you that my cats purr very
　　　　　PLURAL NOUN

_____ , while your dog barks _____ . To conclude, I feel
ADVERB　　　　　　　　　　　　　　　ADVERB

sorry for the _____ -man, who is scared of your _____
　　　　　　　NOUN　　　　　　　　　　　　　　　　　　　ADJECTIVE

dog, while he brings treats for my _____ felines. I'm glad we have
　　　　　　　　　　　　　　　　　ADJECTIVE

been able to come to a/an _____ understanding on this matter.
　　　　　　　　　　　　ADJECTIVE

Yours truly,

The _____ Lady Next Door
　　　ANIMAL

MAD LIBS® is fun to play with friends, but you can also play it by yourself! To begin with, DO NOT look at the story on the page below. Fill in the blanks on this page with the words called for. Then, using the words you have selected, fill in the blank spaces in the story.

Now you've created your own hilarious MAD LIBS® game!

CATS ON CAMERA

ADJECTIVE _____

VERB ENDING IN "ING" _____

NOUN _____

SILLY WORD _____

ADJECTIVE _____

ADJECTIVE _____

NOUN _____

NOUN _____

NOUN _____

EXCLAMATION _____

VERB ENDING IN "S" _____

NOUN _____

ADJECTIVE _____

NUMBER _____

ADJECTIVE _____

PLURAL NOUN _____

MAD LIBS®
CATS ON CAMERA

Cat Lover #1: Have you seen the _____ video on YouTube of the cat
ADJECTIVE

_____ a/an _____?
VERB ENDING IN "ING"   NOUN

Cat Lover #2: _____! It's almost as _____ as that GIF of
SILLY WORD   ADJECTIVE

the _____ kitten playing with a/an _____.
ADJECTIVE   NOUN

Cat Lover #1: And that clip of the _____ cat who pushes her own
NOUN

_____ down some stairs?! _____!
NOUN   EXCLAMATION

Cat Lover #2: How about the cat who _____ along to
VERB ENDING IN "S"

a/an _____ video? Totally _____!
NOUN   ADJECTIVE

Cat Lover #1: And there must be about _____ videos of
NUMBER

_____ cats that have gotten stuck in _____.
ADJECTIVE   PLURAL NOUN

Cat Lover #2: Yep! And I think I've watched them all.

MAD LIBS® is fun to play with friends, but you can also play it by yourself! To begin with, DO NOT look at the story on the page below. Fill in the blanks on this page with the words called for. Then, using the words you have selected, fill in the blank spaces in the story.

Now you've created your own hilarious MAD LIBS® game!

SEVEN SIGNS YOUR CAT LOVES YOU

_____ ADJECTIVE

_____ NOUN

_____ SAME NOUN

_____ PLURAL NOUN

_____ ADJECTIVE

_____ VERB

_____ NOUN

_____ SAME NOUN

_____ ADVERB

_____ NOUN

_____ ADJECTIVE

_____ ANIMAL

_____ A PLACE

_____ ADJECTIVE

MAD LIBS®
SEVEN SIGNS YOUR CAT
LOVES YOU

Here are seven _____ signs your cat loves you:

ADJECTIVE

- Head butting—If your boyfriend or _____ did this to you,

NOUN

  you probably wouldn't want them as your _____ anymore.

SAME NOUN

  But when your cat does it, they are marking you with their facial

  _____, which shows your cat trusts you.

PLURAL NOUN

- Powerful purrs—Cats purr for all kinds of reasons, but that

  _____ body rumble is saved for expressing true love.

ADJECTIVE

- Love bites—If your cat likes to _____ on you, it means they

VERB

  have a serious _____ for you.

NOUN

- Tail twitching—When the tip of a cat's _____ is twitching, it

SAME NOUN

  means they are in total control.

- Tummy up—If your cat rolls around on the ground with its tummy

  showing, it means they trust you _____.

ADVERB

- Kneading—No, your cat doesn't think you are _____ dough;

NOUN

  he is reliving his _____ memories of kittenhood.

ADJECTIVE

- Gifts—You may not want to find a dead _____ in your

ANIMAL

  _____, but this is a/an _____ sign of friendship.

A PLACE · ADJECTIVE

MAD LIBS® is fun to play with friends, but you can also play it by yourself! To begin with, DO NOT look at the story on the page below. Fill in the blanks on this page with the words called for. Then, using the words you have selected, fill in the blank spaces in the story.

Now you've created your own hilarious MAD LIBS® game!

SEVEN SIGNS YOUR CAT IS TRYING TO KILL YOU

_____ ADJECTIVE

_____ PLURAL NOUN

_____ ADVERB

_____ NOUN

_____ PART OF THE BODY

_____ VERB ENDING IN "ING"

_____ ADJECTIVE

_____ PART OF THE BODY

_____ SILLY WORD

_____ NOUN

_____ ADVERB

_____ ANIMAL

_____ ADJECTIVE

There's a flip side to all those ＿＿＿＿＿＿＿＿＿ expressions of love.

ADJECTIVE

- Head butting—Beware! Your cat is not showing you that it trusts you;

  it's telling you that your ＿＿＿＿＿＿＿＿ are numbered!

PLURAL NOUN

- Powerful purrs—This is not a sign of true love; it's ＿＿＿＿＿＿＿＿ a

ADVERB

  battle cry!

- Love bites—Not actually a/an ＿＿＿＿＿＿＿＿ of love, but your cat

NOUN

  tasting you to decide which bit of you to eat first. ＿＿＿＿＿＿＿＿,

PART OF THE BODY

  please!

- Tail twitching—The equivalent of your cat ＿＿＿＿＿＿＿＿ a sword

VERB ENDING IN "ING"

  at you.

- Tummy up—Do not fall for this ＿＿＿＿＿＿＿＿ trick! As soon as

ADJECTIVE

  you put your ＿＿＿＿＿＿＿＿ near your cat's belly, it will scratch the

PART OF THE BODY

  ＿＿＿＿＿＿＿＿ out of it!

SILLY WORD

- Kneading—This is not a/an ＿＿＿＿＿＿＿＿ of affection; your cat is

NOUN

  ＿＿＿＿＿＿＿＿ checking your organs for weaknesses.

ADVERB

- Gifts—A dead ＿＿＿＿＿＿＿＿ is not a gift; it's a/an ＿＿＿＿＿＿＿＿

ANIMAL   ADJECTIVE

  warning. Didn't you see *The Godfather*?!

MAD LIBS® is fun to play with friends, but you can also play it by yourself! To begin with, DO NOT look at the story on the page below. Fill in the blanks on this page with the words called for. Then, using the words you have selected, fill in the blank spaces in the story.

Now you've created your own hilarious MAD LIBS® game!

DOGS VERSUS CATS

ADJECTIVE _____

NOUN _____

ADJECTIVE _____

ADJECTIVE _____

ADJECTIVE _____

PART OF THE BODY (PLURAL) _____

NOUN _____

VERB ENDING IN "ING" _____

NOUN _____

ANIMAL _____

NOUN _____

NOUN _____

ADJECTIVE _____

ADVERB _____

ADJECTIVE _____

MAD☺LIBS®
DOGS VERSUS CATS

If you've ever owned both dogs and cats, you know that the differences between

the two species are _____. They are like night and _____.
                        ADJECTIVE   NOUN

The argument about which pet is more _____ will continue
                                           ADJECTIVE

until the end of time, but it's easy to see why cats are _____.
                                                              ADJECTIVE

For instance, cats won't embarrass you in front of your guests by parading

around with your _____ underwear in their _____.
                    ADJECTIVE   PART OF THE BODY (PLURAL)

Cats are also funnier than dogs, even if they don't know it. And they don't

give a/an _____ if you laugh at them, because they are too busy
              NOUN

_____ their revenge. Cats are natural _____
VERB ENDING IN "ING"   NOUN

repellents—no spider, fly, or _____ stands a chance if there's
                                   ANIMAL

a cat in the _____. Cats have no interest in being hooked up to
                  NOUN

a/an _____ and going for a walk; they'd rather curl up and take
         NOUN

a/an _____ nap. And it's _____ proven that cat owners are
         ADJECTIVE   ADVERB

smarter and more _____ than dog owners. So go get yourself a cat!
                      ADJECTIVE

MAD LIBS® is fun to play with friends, but you can also play it by yourself! To begin with, DO NOT look at the story on the page below. Fill in the blanks on this page with the words called for. Then, using the words you have selected, fill in the blank spaces in the story.

Now you've created your own hilarious MAD LIBS® game!

MY HOUSE, MY RULES.

ADJECTIVE _____

NOUN _____

VERB _____

NOUN _____

SAME NOUN _____

TYPE OF LIQUID _____

VERB ENDING IN "ING" _____

PERSON IN ROOM (FEMALE) _____

VERB _____

SAME VERB _____

ADJECTIVE _____

ADJECTIVE _____

MAD LIBS®
MY HOUSE. MY RULES.

_____ Servant,
   ADJECTIVE

It's quite obvious that you think you control me, but we all know that I am

in charge of this _____. You think I am just a simple cat, but I am
                      NOUN

able to out-_____ you any day of the week. Please be aware that
              VERB

"your" house is actually mine, and I am not to be disturbed if I happen to

be sleeping on your bed or favorite piece of _____. I will scratch
                                                  NOUN

any piece of _____ I want. I do not want to drink _____
                SAME NOUN   TYPE OF LIQUID

from an ordinary bowl; I prefer to lap water from a/an _____
                                                          VERB ENDING IN "ING"

faucet or a toilet. So please remember to leave the toilet seat up—I don't care

what _____ has to say about that. Don't try to get me to
        PERSON IN ROOM (FEMALE)

_____ during the day; you should know better than that. I prefer to
   VERB

_____ at night when you are asleep; this is much more fun. You are
   SAME VERB

a/an _____ human, but you are my human.
        ADJECTIVE

With tolerance,

Your Super-_____ Cat
              ADJECTIVE

MAD LIBS® is fun to play with friends, but you can also play it by yourself! To begin with, DO NOT look at the story on the page below. Fill in the blanks on this page with the words called for. Then, using the words you have selected, fill in the blank spaces in the story.

Now you've created your own hilarious MAD LIBS® game!

AM I IN YOUR WAY?

_____ EXCLAMATION

_____ NOUN

_____ NOUN

_____ ADJECTIVE

_____ NOUN

_____ ADJECTIVE

_____ VERB ENDING IN "ING"

_____ NOUN

_____ VERB ENDING IN "ING"

_____ NOUN

_____ NOUN

_____ VERB

_____ NOUN

_____ TYPE OF FOOD

_____ PART OF THE BODY

MAD LIBS®
AM I IN YOUR WAY?

_____! Were you trying to type? I just felt the need to lie on your
   EXCLAMATION

_____ keyboard at this moment. That _____ you're trying
   NOUN   NOUN

to write isn't as _____ as my nap. Oh, and did you want to read
               ADJECTIVE

today's _____? Tough. It's much more _____ that I use
     NOUN   ADJECTIVE

it as a place to do my _____. And I hope you aren't going to
                     VERB ENDING IN "ING"

do the _____ today, as I am planning on _____ in
        NOUN   VERB ENDING IN "ING"

the laundry _____ all day, and I don't want to be disturbed. Let me
            NOUN

know when you are going to start preparing dinner, as I can help knock things

off the _____. And when you sit down to _____, I will
      NOUN   VERB

certainly expect a few pieces of food from your _____. But please,
                                      NOUN

no _____—you know I turn my _____ up at that.
   TYPE OF FOOD   PART OF THE BODY

MAD LIBS® is fun to play with friends, but you can also play it by yourself! To begin with, DO NOT look at the story on the page below. Fill in the blanks on this page with the words called for. Then, using the words you have selected, fill in the blank spaces in the story.

Now you've created your own hilarious MAD LIBS® game!

THE SEVEN HABITS OF HIGHLY EFFECTIVE KITTENS

PLURAL NOUN _____

ADJECTIVE _____

NOUN _____

VERB ENDING IN "ING" _____

PART OF THE BODY _____

ADJECTIVE _____

VERB _____

ADJECTIVE _____

ANIMAL _____

NOUN _____

ADJECTIVE _____

ANIMAL _____

NOUN _____

NOUN _____

NOUN _____

NOUN _____

VERB _____

All kittens know they must perfect these _____ :
                                          PLURAL NOUN

1. Be as adorably _____ as possible at all times.
                   ADJECTIVE

2. Perfect that tiny, irresistible _____. Your servants will come
                                   NOUN

_____ in a/an _____-beat.
VERB ENDING IN "ING"   PART OF THE BODY

3. Learn the ways of a/an _____ ninja; you can _____
                         ADJECTIVE   VERB

anywhere. It's all about stealth.

4. You must be _____, whether you're facing down the neighbor's
               ADJECTIVE

_____ or jumping off the kitchen _____.
   ANIMAL   NOUN

5. You may be _____, but inside of you beats the heart of
              ADJECTIVE

a/an _____. Honor your heritage.
     ANIMAL

6. Make use of those _____-sharp claws. Climb the living room
                     NOUN

_____ and the Christmas _____ with courage and
   NOUN   NOUN

confidence.

7. And when you sleep, curl up in the tiniest, fluffiest _____ possible.
                                                         NOUN

It will make your servants _____.
                           VERB

MAD LIBS® is fun to play with friends, but you can also play it by yourself! To begin with, DO NOT look at the story on the page below. Fill in the blanks on this page with the words called for. Then, using the words you have selected, fill in the blank spaces in the story.

Now you've created your own hilarious MAD LIBS® game!

YOU CALL THAT CAT FOOD?

EXCLAMATION _____

NOUN _____

ADJECTIVE _____

ANIMAL _____

ADJECTIVE _____

NOUN _____

ADJECTIVE _____

NOUN _____

ADJECTIVE _____

ADJECTIVE _____

NOUN _____

PLURAL NOUN _____

ADJECTIVE _____

NOUN _____

MAD LIBS®
YOU CALL THAT CAT FOOD?

_____! What is this _____ that you put in my bowl? Do
<small>EXCLAMATION</small> <small>NOUN</small>

you really expect me to eat this? Have I not made it perfectly _____
<small>ADJECTIVE</small>

that I prefer fresh _____ to the _____ stuff that comes
<small>ANIMAL</small> <small>ADJECTIVE</small>

out of a/an _____? It looks _____ and smells like a rotting
<small>NOUN</small> <small>ADJECTIVE</small>

_____. And I refuse to eat something that is advertised by a cat who is
<small>NOUN</small>

an embarrassment to my _____ species. Don't get so _____
<small>ADJECTIVE</small> <small>ADJECTIVE</small>

when I jump onto the kitchen _____ to see what you are cooking for
<small>NOUN</small>

yourself—I might not want any of that, either. Some of the _____
<small>PLURAL NOUN</small>

you make look and smell as _____ as that _____ you try
<small>ADJECTIVE</small> <small>NOUN</small>

to feed me!

MAD LIBS® is fun to play with friends, but you can also play it by yourself! To begin with, DO NOT look at the story on the page below. Fill in the blanks on this page with the words called for. Then, using the words you have selected, fill in the blank spaces in the story.

Now you've created your own hilarious MAD LIBS® game!

STRANGE CAT FACTS

VERB ENDING IN "ING" _____

NOUN _____

NUMBER _____

PLURAL NOUN _____

VERB _____

PLURAL NOUN _____

NUMBER _____

NUMBER _____

NOUN _____

NOUN _____

VERB _____

PART OF THE BODY _____

COLOR _____

ADJECTIVE _____

MAD LIBS®
STRANGE CAT FACTS

If you think you know cats, think again:

- On average, cats spend two-thirds of every day _____.
  VERB ENDING IN "ING"

- A group of cats is called a/an "_____."
  NOUN

- A cat can jump up to _____ times its own height in a single
  NUMBER

  bound.

- Cats have over twenty _____ that control their ears.
  PLURAL NOUN

- Cats can't _____ sweetness.
  VERB

- The world's longest cat measured 48.5 _____ long.
  PLURAL NOUN

- A cat has _____ toes on its front paws, but only _____
  NUMBER   NUMBER

  toes on its back paws.

- When a cat leaves its _____ uncovered in the litter box, it is a/
  NOUN

  an _____ of aggression.
  NOUN

- Cats only _____ through their _____ pads.
  VERB   PART OF THE BODY

- _____ cats are bad luck in the United States, but they are
  COLOR

  _____ luck in the United Kingdom and Australia.
  ADJECTIVE

MAD LIBS® is fun to play with friends, but you can also play it by yourself! To begin with, DO NOT look at the story on the page below. Fill in the blanks on this page with the words called for. Then, using the words you have selected, fill in the blank spaces in the story.

Now you've created your own hilarious MAD LIBS® game!

CATS IN A BOX—OR BAG

_____ ADJECTIVE

_____ VERB

_____ ANIMAL (PLURAL)

_____ PLURAL NOUN

_____ ADJECTIVE

_____ ADJECTIVE

_____ ARTICLE OF CLOTHING

_____ PLURAL NOUN

_____ VERB

_____ SAME VERB

_____ ADJECTIVE

_____ NOUN

_____ PLURAL NOUN

_____ ADJECTIVE

_____ ANIMAL (PLURAL)

_____ VERB

MAD LIBS
CATS IN A BOX—OR BAG

Don't bother buying me some _____ toy; I won't _____ with it. So
                        ADJECTIVE   VERB

skip the fake _____ filled with catnip and those "teasers" with
               ANIMAL (PLURAL)

_____ on the ends. Just give me an old _____ box. The secret
PLURAL NOUN   ADJECTIVE

of the old _____ box is that it gives me (a/an) _____
            ADJECTIVE   ARTICLE OF CLOTHING

of invisibility, enhancing my super-_____. When I am in the box,
                             PLURAL NOUN

I can _____ you, but you can't _____ me. If the box is
        VERB   SAME VERB

_____, that's even better, as it is more fun if I can barely get myself in
ADJECTIVE

it. And it is preferable if the box has a/an _____ or _____.
                                 NOUN   PLURAL NOUN

And if you don't have a box, a/an _____ paper bag will do. Because
                            ADJECTIVE

within the bag live the Bag _____. And it is my mission in life
                        ANIMAL (PLURAL)

to _____ them!
   VERB

MAD LIBS® is fun to play with friends, but you can also play it by yourself! To begin with, DO NOT look at the story on the page below. Fill in the blanks on this page with the words called for. Then, using the words you have selected, fill in the blank spaces in the story.

Now you've created your own hilarious MAD LIBS® game!

BIG CATS

_____ VERB

_____ PLURAL NOUN

_____ PLURAL NOUN

_____ ADJECTIVE

_____ ADJECTIVE

_____ ANIMAL

_____ SAME ANIMAL

_____ ADJECTIVE

_____ ADJECTIVE

_____ VERB

_____ SAME VERB

_____ ADJECTIVE

_____ VERB ENDING IN "ING"

_____ SAME VERB ENDING IN "ING"

_____ A PLACE

_____ ADJECTIVE

_____ NOUN

_____ ADJECTIVE

MAD LIBS
BIG CATS

Although they don't have to _____ for their food or worry about
                            VERB

_____, domestic cats aren't all that different from their wild
PLURAL NOUN

_____ and sisters. All cats, domestic and _____, are
PLURAL NOUN   ADJECTIVE

_____ carnivores, whether they prefer to eat a can of _____
ADJECTIVE   ANIMAL

delight or an entire raw _____. Felines around the world, from
                         SAME ANIMAL

_____ tabbies to _____ jaguars, _____ for sixteen to
ADJECTIVE   ADJECTIVE   VERB

twenty hours a day. (However, snow leopards don't get to _____
                                                         SAME VERB

in a basket of _____ laundry.) And there's the _____
               ADJECTIVE   VERB ENDING IN "ING"

thing. You might think your cat is _____ against you
                                   SAME VERB ENDING IN "ING"

because it loves you. But it's marking you, just like big cats mark their territory

in (the) _____. And even though there are _____
         A PLACE   ADJECTIVE

similarities between a house cat and a cheetah, it's much safer to have a domestic

cat in your _____—so don't get any _____ ideas!
            NOUN   ADJECTIVE

CATS IN BOOKS

_____ ADJECTIVE

_____ ADJECTIVE

_____ VERB ENDING IN "ING"

_____ ADJECTIVE

_____ PERSON IN ROOM (MALE)

_____ PART OF THE BODY

_____ PERSON IN ROOM (MALE)

_____ A PLACE

_____ ADJECTIVE

_____ ADJECTIVE

_____ PLURAL NOUN

_____ PART OF THE BODY

_____ ADJECTIVE

_____ PLURAL NOUN

_____ ADJECTIVE

_____ PART OF THE BODY

MAD LIBS®
CATS IN BOOKS

Test your knowledge about cats who have made their _____ mark in
ADJECTIVE

literature:

- The cat who seems to be _____ and can't stop
  ADJECTIVE

  _____ at Alice: The Cheshire Cat
  VERB ENDING IN "ING"

- The _____ cat in _____ King's horror
  ADJECTIVE PERSON IN ROOM (MALE)

  classic: Church

- The cat with a squashed _____ who belongs to
  PART OF THE BODY

  _____ Potter's best friend: Crookshanks
  PERSON IN ROOM (MALE)

- The _____ cat who is the best friend of the _____
  A PLACE ADJECTIVE

  cockroach Archy: Mehitabel

- A mysterious, _____, and small black cat capable of
  ADJECTIVE

  performing _____ of magic and sleight of _____:
  PLURAL NOUN PART OF THE BODY

  Mr. Mistoffelees

- The story of a very _____ kitten who struggles to keep his
  ADJECTIVE

  _____ clean and tidy: *Tom Kitten*
  PLURAL NOUN

- A/An _____ tale about a cat who wins the _____
  ADJECTIVE PART OF THE BODY

  of a princess in marriage: *Puss in Boots*

MAD LIBS® is fun to play with friends, but you can also play it by yourself! To begin with, DO NOT look at the story on the page below. Fill in the blanks on this page with the words called for. Then, using the words you have selected, fill in the blank spaces in the story.

Now you've created your own hilarious MAD LIBS® game!

DRESSING YOUR CAT

ADJECTIVE _____

NOUN _____

PART OF THE BODY (PLURAL) _____

ANIMAL _____

ADJECTIVE _____

PERSON IN ROOM (MALE) _____

COLOR _____

PLURAL NOUN _____

OCCUPATION _____

NOUN _____

NOUN _____

ARTICLE OF CLOTHING _____

ADJECTIVE _____

NOUN _____

ADVERB _____

ADJECTIVE _____

MAD LIBS
DRESSING YOUR CAT

Your cat can help you celebrate your favorite holidays throughout the year. All

you need to do is dress it up in a/an _____, fun _____.
ADJECTIVE   NOUN

With a pair of fuzzy _____, your cat can be transformed
PART OF THE BODY (PLURAL)

into the Easter _____. Or be _____ and turn your
ANIMAL   ADJECTIVE

cat into Uncle _____ with a little red, white, and
PERSON IN ROOM (MALE)

_____ suit. And there are a lot of _____ for your cat to wear
COLOR   PLURAL NOUN

on Halloween. You can dress your cat as a/an _____ in a pink tutu,
OCCUPATION

a prehistoric _____ with spikes down its back, or a superhero like
NOUN

_____-man with a black cape and matching _____.
NOUN   ARTICLE OF CLOTHING

And of course any cat can be turned into Santa Claus with a/an _____
ADJECTIVE

red suit and a cute matching _____. Just make sure you choose
NOUN

_____—you don't want to get on your cat's _____ side!
ADVERB   ADJECTIVE

NINE LIVES

NOUN _____

ADJECTIVE _____

VERB ENDING IN "ING" _____

ADJECTIVE _____

ADJECTIVE _____

ANIMAL _____

ADJECTIVE _____

NOUN _____

NUMBER _____

TYPE OF LIQUID _____

NOUN _____

VERB (PAST TENSE) _____

NOUN _____

ADJECTIVE _____

VEHICLE _____

NOUN _____

NOUN _____

ADJECTIVE _____

MAD LIBS® is fun to play with friends, but you can also play it by yourself! To begin with, DO NOT look at the story on the page below. Fill in the blanks on this page with the words called for. Then, using the words you have selected, fill in the blank spaces in the story.

Now you've created your own hilarious MAD LIBS® game!

MAD LIBS
NINE LIVES

Life #1—I ate a/an _____ — a/an _____ mistake.
NOUN ADJECTIVE

Life #2—I didn't look both ways before _____ the street.
VERB ENDING IN "ING"

_____ move.
ADJECTIVE

Life #3—I was a bit too _____ when I teased the neighbor's
ADJECTIVE

_____ .
ANIMAL

Life #4—I thought cats were supposed to be able to survive falls from

_____ places?!
ADJECTIVE

Life #5—I got locked in the _____ for _____ days without
NOUN NUMBER

food or _____. What's a/an _____ to do?!
TYPE OF LIQUID NOUN

Life #6—I _____ into the washing machine. That spin cycle is a
VERB (PAST TENSE)

killer, let me tell you . . .

Life #7—I chewed through the cord to the _____. That was
NOUN

a/an _____ shocker.
ADJECTIVE

Life #8—I was keeping warm under the _____ when my human
VEHICLE

decided to start it. I should have just taken a nap in the _____ basket.
NOUN

I have one _____ left—better make it _____!
NOUN ADJECTIVE

MADLIBS®

UNICORNS, MERMAIDS, AND MAD LIBS

by Billy Merrell

Mad Libs
An Imprint of Penguin Random House

MAD LIBS®

INSTRUCTIONS

MAD LIBS® is a game for people who don't like games!
It can be played by one, two, three, four, or forty.

•RIDICULOUSLY SIMPLE DIRECTIONS

In this tablet you will find stories containing blank spaces where words are left out. One player, the READER, selects one of these stories. The READER does not tell anyone what the story is about. Instead, he/she asks the other players, the WRITERS, to give him/her words. These words are used to fill in the blank spaces in the story.

•TO PLAY

The READER asks each WRITER in turn to call out a word—an adjective or a noun or whatever the space calls for—and uses them to fill in the blank spaces in the story. The result is a MAD LIBS® game.

When the READER then reads the completed MAD LIBS® game to the other players, they will discover that they have written a story that is fantastic, screamingly funny, shocking, silly, crazy, or just plain dumb—depending upon which words each WRITER called out.

•EXAMPLE (*Before* and *After*)

"_____!" he said _____
      EXCLAMATION   ADVERB

as he jumped into his convertible _____ and
                                    NOUN

drove off with his _____ wife.
                   ADJECTIVE

"_____OUCH_____!" he said _____STUPIDLY_____
      EXCLAMATION   ADVERB

as he jumped into his convertible _____CAT_____ and
                                    NOUN

drove off with his _____BRAVE_____ wife.
                   ADJECTIVE

MAD LIBS®

QUICK REVIEW

In case you have forgotten what adjectives, adverbs, nouns, and verbs are, here is a quick review:

An ADJECTIVE describes something or somebody. *Lumpy, soft, ugly, messy,* and *short* are adjectives.

An ADVERB tells how something is done. It modifies a verb and usually ends in "ly." *Modestly, stupidly, greedily,* and *carefully* are adverbs.

A NOUN is the name of a person, place, or thing. *Sidewalk, umbrella, bridle, bathtub,* and *nose* are nouns.

A VERB is an action word. *Run, pitch, jump,* and *swim* are verbs. Put the verbs in past tense if the directions say PAST TENSE. *Ran, pitched, jumped,* and *swam* are verbs in the past tense.

When we ask for A PLACE, we mean any sort of place: a country or city *(Spain, Cleveland)* or a room *(bathroom, kitchen).*

An EXCLAMATION or SILLY WORD is any sort of funny sound, gasp, grunt, or outcry, like *Wow!, Ouch!, Whomp!, Ick!,* and *Gadzooks!*

When we ask for specific words, like a NUMBER, a COLOR, an ANIMAL, or a PART OF THE BODY, we mean a word that is one of those things, like *seven, blue, horse,* or *head.*

When we ask for a PLURAL, it means more than one. For example, *cat* pluralized is *cats.*

MAD LIBS® is fun to play with friends, but you can also play it by yourself! To begin with, DO NOT look at the story on the page below. Fill in the blanks on this page with the words called for. Then, using the words you have selected, fill in the blank spaces in the story.

Now you've created your own hilarious MAD LIBS® game!

HOW TO HATCH A DRAGON EGG

ADJECTIVE _____

PLURAL NOUN _____

PLURAL NOUN _____

COLOR _____

NUMBER _____

VERB _____

TYPE OF LIQUID _____

ADJECTIVE _____

PLURAL NOUN _____

NUMBER _____

ADJECTIVE _____

NOUN _____

SILLY WORD _____

A PLACE _____

ADJECTIVE _____

NOUN _____

VERB ENDING IN "ING" _____

PART OF THE BODY (PLURAL) _____

While most eggs need _____ love and care for the _____
ADJECTIVE   PLURAL NOUN

inside to survive, dragon eggs thrive on danger! In fact, the _____
PLURAL NOUN

of _____ dragons *require* a/an _____-foot drop in order to
COLOR   NUMBER

_____ open. Eggs of _____ dragons depend on
VERB   TYPE OF LIQUID

_____ lava from underwater _____ to heat the shells to
ADJECTIVE   PLURAL NOUN

temperatures of _____ degrees or more. Only then can the _____
NUMBER   ADJECTIVE

dragonets inside finally hatch. But the _____ of the skies,
NOUN

the _____ dragon of (the) _____, is the most _____
SILLY WORD   A PLACE   ADJECTIVE

_____-layer of them all! They have been spotted
NOUN

_____ into the _____ of hungry predators,
VERB ENDING IN "ING"   PART OF THE BODY (PLURAL)

hoping to be swallowed. Once they hatch, they cause quite a bellyache!

MAD LIBS® is fun to play with friends, but you can also play it by yourself! To begin with, DO NOT look at the story on the page below. Fill in the blanks on this page with the words called for. Then, using the words you have selected, fill in the blank spaces in the story.

Now you've created your own hilarious MAD LIBS® game!

WHAT UNICORNS EAT

PLURAL NOUN _____

ADJECTIVE _____

NOUN _____

TYPE OF FOOD _____

ARTICLE OF CLOTHING (PLURAL) _____

VERB ENDING IN "ING" _____

PLURAL NOUN _____

PLURAL NOUN _____

NUMBER _____

CELEBRITY (FEMALE) _____

COLOR _____

VERB ENDING IN "ING" _____

TYPE OF FOOD (PLURAL) _____

PLURAL NOUN _____

ADJECTIVE _____

ADJECTIVE _____

Would it surprise you to learn that the most majestic _____ in the
_____PLURAL NOUN

world eat garbage? Well, they do! Everything from _____
_____ADJECTIVE

soda cans to _____-stained _____ boxes to used
_____NOUN_____TYPE OF FOOD

_____—and more! Some have been spotted
ARTICLE OF CLOTHING (PLURAL)

_____ dumpsters and then using their long _____
VERB ENDING IN "ING"_____PLURAL NOUN

to spear as many bags of _____ as they can before being caught.
_____PLURAL NOUN

According to an interview with _____ *Minutes,* _____
_____NUMBER_____CELEBRITY (FEMALE)

once came home to find a/an _____ unicorn _____
_____COLOR_____VERB ENDING IN "ING"

up in her recycling bin. The poor thing had mistaken her husband's leftover

_____ for dried-up _____. "It was a/an _____
TYPE OF FOOD (PLURAL)_____PLURAL NOUN_____ADJECTIVE

mistake," she said. "My husband is a/an _____ cook!"
_____ADJECTIVE

BAD HOUSEKEEPING

NOUN _____

ADJECTIVE _____

NOUN _____

PLURAL NOUN _____

VERB ENDING IN "ING" _____

PLURAL NOUN _____

NOUN _____

PLURAL NOUN _____

TYPE OF FOOD _____

NOUN _____

SILLY WORD _____

A PLACE _____

NUMBER _____

NOUN _____

SAME NOUN _____

MAD LIBS® is fun to play with friends, but you can also play it by yourself! To begin with, DO NOT look at the story on the page below. Fill in the blanks on this page with the words called for. Then, using the words you have selected, fill in the blank spaces in the story.

Now you've created your own hilarious MAD LIBS® game!

MAD LIBS®
BAD HOUSEKEEPING

The troll that lives under the _____ shares tips for keeping his home

NOUN

_____ clean.

ADJECTIVE

- **Decorate sparingly.** Don't clutter up your _____

NOUN

with sentimental garbage, like pictures of _____ or

PLURAL NOUN

_____ trophies. Having too many _____

VERB ENDING IN "ING"   PLURAL NOUN

visible ruins the element of surprise!

- **Clean up immediately.** It's easy to let _____-work get

NOUN

away from you. Wash the _____ right after meals, so that

PLURAL NOUN

_____ doesn't sit too long in the sink. For a troll, scraps of

TYPE OF FOOD

_____ could be considered evidence!

NOUN

- **Make the most of it.** Even if it doesn't win the _____ award

SILLY WORD

for best home in (the) _____, it's still yours! Spend at least

A PLACE

_____ minutes a day simply sitting back and appreciating your

NUMBER

" _____ , sweet _____ ."

NOUN   SAME NOUN

MAD LIBS® is fun to play with friends, but you can also play it by yourself! To begin with, DO NOT look at the story on the page below. Fill in the blanks on this page with the words called for. Then, using the words you have selected, fill in the blank spaces in the story.

Now you've created your own hilarious MAD LIBS® game!

ENCOUNTER WITH BIGFOOT

NOUN _____

A PLACE _____

PART OF THE BODY _____

NOUN _____

ADJECTIVE _____

ADJECTIVE _____

PART OF THE BODY (PLURAL) _____

ADJECTIVE _____

ADJECTIVE _____

TYPE OF FOOD _____

VERB ENDING IN "ING" _____

ANIMAL _____

PART OF THE BODY (PLURAL) _____

VERB ENDING IN "ING" _____

CELEBRITY _____

NOUN _____

TYPE OF LIQUID _____

TYPE OF FOOD _____

MAD☺LIBS®
ENCOUNTER WITH BIGFOOT

Before they vanished, a well-trained _____ of explorers sent an SOS
NOUN

from the snowy peaks of (the) _____, claiming to have spotted Big-
A PLACE

_____. This is what their _____ said:
PART OF THE BODY   NOUN

OMG, he's real. I'm looking at _____-foot right now. And he's
ADJECTIVE

_____! I've never seen such human _____ on a
ADJECTIVE   PART OF THE BODY (PLURAL)

creature so _____! At first he looked as _____ as we all were.
ADJECTIVE   ADJECTIVE

But as we approached, he became cool as a/an _____, silently
TYPE OF FOOD

_____ us. "What's the matter?" I said. "_____
VERB ENDING IN "ING"   ANIMAL

got your tongue?" But we couldn't believe our _____—he
PART OF THE BODY (PLURAL)

actually spoke! Now the creature won't stop _____ on and on
VERB ENDING IN "ING"

about _____ and _____-flavored _____.
CELEBRITY   NOUN   TYPE OF LIQUID

Help! Someone make this beast shut his _____-hole!
TYPE OF FOOD

MAD LIBS® is fun to play with friends, but you can also play it by yourself! To begin with, DO NOT look at the story on the page below. Fill in the blanks on this page with the words called for. Then, using the words you have selected, fill in the blank spaces in the story.

Now you've created your own hilarious MAD LIBS® game!

A-MAZE-ING MINOTAUR

ANIMAL _____

NOUN _____

PLURAL NOUN _____

ADJECTIVE _____

VERB _____

ADJECTIVE _____

PLURAL NOUN _____

VERB _____

ADJECTIVE _____

PART OF THE BODY (PLURAL) _____

PLURAL NOUN _____

NOUN _____

PLURAL NOUN _____

ADJECTIVE _____

NOUN _____

ANIMAL _____

MAD LIBS®
A-MAZE-ING MINOTAUR

Interviewer: So, what's it like having a/an _____ head, but a human
<u>ANIMAL</u>

_____?
<u>NOUN</u>

Mini: It's just about what you'd expect. _____ don't take me
<u>PLURAL NOUN</u>

seriously. My therapist misses every _____ appointment. I could
<u>ADJECTIVE</u>

_____!
<u>VERB</u>

Interviewer: How unfortunate! Do you think they are _____ against
<u>ADJECTIVE</u>

all non-_____, or what?
<u>PLURAL NOUN</u>

Mini: I do hunt and _____ people I find wandering lost inside the maze.
<u>VERB</u>

That could be the reason for the _____ look in their
<u>ADJECTIVE</u>

_____.
<u>PART OF THE BODY (PLURAL)</u>

Interviewer: That seems likely. After all, _____ speak louder than
<u>PLURAL NOUN</u>

words. With that in _____, do you have anything to say to the families
<u>NOUN</u>

of your _____?
<u>PLURAL NOUN</u>

Mini: Only that it's never _____ to judge a book by its _____.
<u>ADJECTIVE</u>   <u>NOUN</u>

Despite my looks, on the inside I have the heart of a/an _____.
<u>ANIMAL</u>

MAD LIBS® is fun to play with friends, but you can also play it by yourself! To begin with, DO NOT look at the story on the page below. Fill in the blanks on this page with the words called for. Then, using the words you have selected, fill in the blank spaces in the story.

Now you've created your own hilarious MAD LIBS® game!

A GENIE'S CONTRACT

ADJECTIVE _____

VERB ENDING IN "ING" _____

NUMBER _____

NOUN _____

NUMBER _____

NOUN _____

NOUN _____

ADJECTIVE _____

A PLACE _____

NUMBER _____

ADJECTIVE _____

VERB _____

VERB _____

NOUN _____

NOUN _____

PLURAL NOUN _____

ADVERB _____

Be sure to read the _____ print:
ADJECTIVE

The individual responsible for _____ the lamp is entitled to
VERB ENDING IN "ING"

_____ wishes, to be granted by the _____ inside. Limit
NUMBER _NOUN_

_____ wishes per master, or one (1) _____ per day. At the genie's
NUMBER _NOUN_

discretion, a/an _____ may be substituted for a lamp at any time.
NOUN

Offer only _____ at participating locations, excluding (the)
ADJECTIVE

_____. Official wishes must be limited to _____ characters, in
A PLACE _NUMBER_

order to minimize _____ consequences that may _____ due
ADJECTIVE _VERB_

to unnecessary verbosity. May not be used to make a person _____ in love
VERB

or combined with any other _____ or offer. The lamp (or substituted
NOUN

_____) must be surrendered after the final wish. Wishing for more
NOUN

_____ is _____ prohibited.
PLURAL NOUN _ADVERB_

MAD LIBS® is fun to play with friends, but you can also play it by yourself! To begin with, DO NOT look at the story on the page below. Fill in the blanks on this page with the words called for. Then, using the words you have selected, fill in the blank spaces in the story.

Now you've created your own hilarious MAD LIBS® game!

WHY GIANTS DON'T SLEEP

VERB _____

NUMBER _____

ADJECTIVE _____

ADJECTIVE _____

EXCLAMATION _____

PART OF THE BODY _____

PART OF THE BODY _____

ADJECTIVE _____

PLURAL NOUN _____

VERB _____

COLOR _____

TYPE OF LIQUID _____

PLURAL NOUN _____

ADVERB _____

VERB ENDING IN "ING" _____

ANIMAL _____

ARTICLE OF CLOTHING (PLURAL) _____

Finding a place to sit and _____ when you're more than _____
                          VERB   NUMBER

feet tall is no _____ task. And lying down is next to _____!
                 ADJECTIVE   ADJECTIVE

_____! It would take an area the size of two _____-ball fields
 EXCLAMATION   PART OF THE BODY

for a giant to stretch out from head to _____. That's why, for a giant,
                                          PART OF THE BODY

waking up on the _____ side of the bed is all but inevitable. The
                   ADJECTIVE

closest that most _____ get to a comfortable place to _____
                   PLURAL NOUN   VERB

are bogs, where _____ mud, _____, and dead
                 COLOR   TYPE OF LIQUID

_____ form a kind of mattress. And even there, they must take care
 PLURAL NOUN

not to sleep too _____, or else they risk _____
                  ADVERB   VERB ENDING IN "ING"

in the mud and drowning. Besides, most giants would rather chug Red

_____ all night than get mud on their _____.
 ANIMAL   ARTICLE OF CLOTHING (PLURAL)

MAD LIBS® is fun to play with friends, but you can also play it by yourself! To begin with, DO NOT look at the story on the page below. Fill in the blanks on this page with the words called for. Then, using the words you have selected, fill in the blank spaces in the story.

Now you've created your own hilarious MAD LIBS® game!

CERBERUS TRAINING

PERSON IN ROOM (MALE) _____

NUMBER _____

ANIMAL _____

PLURAL NOUN _____

SILLY WORD _____

NOUN _____

VERB _____

VERB _____

TYPE OF FOOD _____

PART OF THE BODY (PLURAL) _____

VERB _____

PART OF THE BODY _____

ADJECTIVE _____

ADVERB _____

PLURAL NOUN _____

ADJECTIVE _____

VERB _____

NOUN _____

VERB ENDING IN "ING" _____

MAD LIBS®
CERBERUS TRAINING

Here are some tips for training _____, your _____-headed
                                 PERSON IN ROOM (MALE)   NUMBER

guard _____.
        ANIMAL

1. **Be consistent.** The same _____ and commands should always
                                PLURAL NOUN

   apply.

2. **Be concise.** Don't say _____ several times in a/an _____,
                             SILLY WORD   NOUN

   or else he'll _____ the word out entirely.
                  VERB

3. **Be generous.** _____ him for being right by giving him treats,
                     VERB

   like _____—yes, one for each of his _____.
        TYPE OF FOOD   PART OF THE BODY (PLURAL)

   But don't over-_____ him! Verbal praise and _____
                    VERB   PART OF THE BODY

   massages can serve as _____ reinforcement, too.
                          ADJECTIVE

4. **Be patient.** Understand that training him _____ takes time.
                                                 ADVERB

   Don't expect immediate _____. Take a/an _____ tone
                           PLURAL NOUN   ADJECTIVE

   and _____ at him so he knows you're on his _____.
        VERB   NOUN

5. **Lastly, enjoy!** Make sure you both have a good time, and he'll be

   _____ out of your hand in no time.
   VERB ENDING IN "ING"

MAD LIBS® is fun to play with friends, but you can also play it by yourself! To begin with, DO NOT look at the story on the page below. Fill in the blanks on this page with the words called for. Then, using the words you have selected, fill in the blank spaces in the story.

Now you've created your own hilarious MAD LIBS® game!

PEGASUS BREAKS GROUND

_____ ANIMAL

_____ OCCUPATION

_____ VERB ENDING IN "ING"

_____ A PLACE

_____ PERSON IN ROOM (FEMALE)

_____ PART OF THE BODY (PLURAL)

_____ TYPE OF LIQUID

_____ NOUN

_____ NUMBER

_____ A PLACE

_____ CELEBRITY (MALE)

_____ NUMBER

_____ CELEBRITY (FEMALE)

_____ NOUN

_____ SILLY WORD

_____ VERB ENDING IN "ING"

_____ ADJECTIVE

MAD LIBS
PEGASUS BREAKS GROUND

Breaking news! A flying _____ escaped from his _____ today
_{ANIMAL} _{OCCUPATION}

while _____ for the Muses in (the) _____. According
_{VERB ENDING IN "ING"} _{A PLACE}

to the witness, _____, when the creature dug his
_{PERSON IN ROOM (FEMALE)}

_____ into the soil, a spring of _____ bubbled
_{PART OF THE BODY (PLURAL)} _{TYPE OF LIQUID}

up from the ground, forming a/an _____-clear fountain. For the past
_{NOUN}

_____ hours, Muses from as far away as (the) _____ have come
_{NUMBER} _{A PLACE}

to see the miracle for themselves. _____ offered to buy the
_{CELEBRITY (MALE)}

creature for _____ dollars, but _____, backed by a
_{NUMBER} _{CELEBRITY (FEMALE)}

crowd of _____-rights activists, insisted the animal isn't for sale. In
_{NOUN}

related news, the _____ Corporation has already bought
_{SILLY WORD}

_____ rights for the fountain and has plans to create a new
_{VERB ENDING IN "ING"}

_____ drink with Pegasus as their mascot.
_{ADJECTIVE}

MAD LIBS® is fun to play with friends, but you can also play it by yourself! To begin with, DO NOT look at the story on the page below. Fill in the blanks on this page with the words called for. Then, using the words you have selected, fill in the blank spaces in the story.

Now you've created your own hilarious MAD LIBS® game!

COOKING WITH MERMAIDS

PERSON IN ROOM (FEMALE) _____

NUMBER _____

ADJECTIVE _____

NOUN _____

ANIMAL _____

TYPE OF LIQUID _____

NUMBER _____

VERB _____

ADVERB _____

COLOR _____

NUMBER _____

NOUN _____

ADJECTIVE _____

ADJECTIVE _____

PLURAL NOUN _____

VERB ENDING IN "ING" _____

ADJECTIVE _____

A PLACE _____

MAD LIBS®
COOKING WITH MERMAIDS

Here is a recipe for Kraken eggs, from _____'s Underwater
                                        PERSON IN ROOM (FEMALE)

Kitchen. (Serves _____)
                  NUMBER

Ingredients:

1 _____ egg, stolen from a giant Kraken
   ADJECTIVE

4 _____-spoons _____ milk (fresh if possible)
   NOUN   ANIMAL

3 _____-spoons squid ink
   TYPE OF LIQUID

_____ sea urchins (for garnish)
 NUMBER

Directions:

_____ the first three ingredients. Beat _____ until the
 VERB   ADVERB

mixture turns _____ and frothy, about _____ minutes. Using a
               COLOR   NUMBER

pastry _____, pipe _____ portions of egg batter into a/an
        NOUN   ADJECTIVE

_____ tide pool. Allow the _____ to cook for four minutes,
 ADJECTIVE   PLURAL NOUN

_____ them in a net as you go. Serve alongside the
 VERB ENDING IN "ING"

_____ urchins. Season with _____ water, to taste.
 ADJECTIVE   A PLACE

MYTHICAL MONSTERS IN HISTORY

_____
NOUN

_____
PART OF THE BODY

_____
ANIMAL (PLURAL)

_____
NOUN

_____
PART OF THE BODY (PLURAL)

_____
NOUN

_____
ADJECTIVE

_____
ADJECTIVE

_____
VERB ENDING IN "ING"

_____
NOUN

_____
PERSON IN ROOM (FEMALE)

_____
ANIMAL

_____
NOUN

_____
TYPE OF LIQUID

_____
ADVERB

_____
PLURAL NOUN

_____
NUMBER

MAD LIBS® is fun to play with friends, but you can also play it by yourself! To begin with, DO NOT look at the story on the page below. Fill in the blanks on this page with the words called for. Then, using the words you have selected, fill in the blank spaces in the story.

Now you've created your own hilarious MAD LIBS® game!

MAD LIBS®
MYTHICAL MONSTERS
IN HISTORY

- **Medusa** was a/an _____ with a hideous _____ and
  <small>NOUN</small> <small>PART OF THE BODY</small>

  venomous _____ for hair. According to _____
  <small>ANIMAL (PLURAL)</small> <small>NOUN</small>

  mythology, looking into Medusa's _____ could turn
  <small>PART OF THE BODY (PLURAL)</small>

  you to _____.
  <small>NOUN</small>

- **Arachne** was born a/an _____ human woman with
  <small>ADJECTIVE</small>

  nothing extra-_____ about her—aside from her talent for
  <small>ADJECTIVE</small>

  _____. After winning a/an _____ against
  <small>VERB ENDING IN "ING"</small> <small>NOUN</small>

  the goddess _____, Arachne was turned into a/an
  <small>PERSON IN ROOM (FEMALE)</small>

  _____.
  <small>ANIMAL</small>

- **The Loch Ness** _____ is a famous "_____ beast"
  <small>NOUN</small> <small>TYPE OF LIQUID</small>

  living in a Scottish lake. "Nessie," as the creature has been _____
  <small>ADVERB</small>

  nicknamed, supposedly appeared on satellite _____ as
  <small>PLURAL NOUN</small>

  recently as _____ years ago.
  <small>NUMBER</small>

MAD LIBS® is fun to play with friends, but you can also play it by yourself! To begin with, DO NOT look at the story on the page below. Fill in the blanks on this page with the words called for. Then, using the words you have selected, fill in the blank spaces in the story.

Now you've created your own hilarious MAD LIBS® game!

LAKE MONSTERS OF NORTH AMERICA

_____ VERB

_____ A PLACE

_____ NOUN

_____ PLURAL NOUN

_____ NUMBER

_____ TYPE OF LIQUID

_____ PLURAL NOUN

_____ ANIMAL

_____ ADJECTIVE

_____ PART OF THE BODY (PLURAL)

_____ ANIMAL

_____ PART OF THE BODY

_____ NOUN

_____ ANIMAL

_____ FIRST NAME

_____ NUMBER

Why _____ all the way to (the) _____ when there are
    VERB   A PLACE

_____ monsters right here at home? Between the United
  NOUN

_____ and Canada, North America is home to more than
  PLURAL NOUN

_____ lake and river monsters, like giant _____ serpents,
  NUMBER   TYPE OF LIQUID

crocodilian _____, and _____-like fish with _____
    PLURAL NOUN   ANIMAL   ADJECTIVE

necks and webbed _____. Ontario was once home to
        PART OF THE BODY (PLURAL)

Mishipeshu, an "underwater _____" with a catlike _____ and
        ANIMAL   PART OF THE BODY

claws. And British Columbia is still home to Ogopogo, a/an _____-
                NOUN

backed creature with a bearded _____ head. But Canada's favorite
         ANIMAL

just might be "_____," which has been described as looking
    FIRST NAME

somewhat like a/an _____-eyed Loch Ness Monster.
      NUMBER

MAD LIBS® is fun to play with friends, but you can also play it by yourself! To begin with, DO NOT look at the story on the page below. Fill in the blanks on this page with the words called for. Then, using the words you have selected, fill in the blank spaces in the story.

Now you've created your own hilarious MAD LIBS® game!

MOST FAMOUS MERMAIDS

ADJECTIVE _____

ADJECTIVE _____

VERB _____

PLURAL NOUN _____

NOUN _____

PERSON IN ROOM (MALE) _____

SILLY WORD _____

VERB ENDING IN "ING" _____

A PLACE _____

ADVERB _____

OCCUPATION (PLURAL) _____

NUMBER _____

ADJECTIVE _____

PERSON IN ROOM (FEMALE) _____

ADJECTIVE _____

NOUN _____

LAST NAME _____

NOUN _____

NOUN _____

MAD LIBS

MOST FAMOUS MERMAIDS

Here is a list of some of the most _____ mermaids in history.
_{ADJECTIVE}

- The Sirens of Greek mythology were _____ but
_{ADJECTIVE}

  dangerous creatures who would _____ sailors with their
  _{VERB}

  _____, causing _____-wrecks. They appear in
  _{PLURAL NOUN} _{NOUN}

  both _____'s *Odyssey* and Ovid's _____.
  _{PERSON IN ROOM (MALE)} _{SILLY WORD}

- The _____ mermaids of Weeki Wachee Springs in (the)
_{VERB ENDING IN "ING"}

  _____ are _____ famous. In the 1960s, these female
  _{A PLACE} _{ADVERB}

  _____ drew nearly _____ tourists per year!
  _{OCCUPATION (PLURAL)} _{NUMBER}

- The most _____ mermaid in the world is probably
_{ADJECTIVE}

  _____, the main character of the animated film
  _{PERSON IN ROOM (FEMALE)}

  The _____ *Mermaid*. Based on the _____ tale by
  _{ADJECTIVE} _{NOUN}

  Hans Christian _____, the film tells the story of a teenage
  _{LAST NAME}

  _____ who is willing to do whatever it takes to become human.
  _{NOUN}

  Even if it means losing her _____!
  _{NOUN}

FAERY SIGHTINGS ON THE RISE

_____
NOUN

_____
VERB

_____
NOUN

_____
PLURAL NOUN

_____
NOUN

_____
LAST NAME

_____
OCCUPATION

_____
PLURAL NOUN

_____
NUMBER

_____
ADVERB

_____
ADJECTIVE

_____
VERB

_____
ADJECTIVE

_____
PART OF THE BODY

_____
PLURAL NOUN

_____
NOUN

_____
NUMBER

MAD LIBS®
FAERY SIGHTINGS
ON THE RISE

Since at least 1927, the Faery Investigation _____ has met to
                                              NOUN
_____ and gather evidence of _____ life in all its reported
   VERB   NOUN

forms. In the Society's heyday, it boasted several famous _____,
                                                          PLURAL NOUN

including decorated _____ hero Lord _____ and iconic
                       NOUN   LAST NAME

_____ Walt Disney. Though many of their _____ were
 OCCUPATION   PLURAL NOUN

destroyed during World War _____, the Society grew _____
                            NUMBER   ADVERB

over the decades, until _____ ridicule in the '90s drove the Society to
                          ADJECTIVE

_____ underground. Today, however, they appear to be as
   VERB

_____ as ever, with an active _____-book page and hundreds
 ADJECTIVE   PART OF THE BODY

of devoted _____. A recent census conducted by the Society shows
            PLURAL NOUN

_____ sightings are on the rise, with _____ occurring in the past
   NOUN   NUMBER

year alone.

MAD LIBS® is fun to play with friends, but you can also play it by yourself! To begin with, DO NOT look at the story on the page below. Fill in the blanks on this page with the words called for. Then, using the words you have selected, fill in the blank spaces in the story.

Now you've created your own hilarious MAD LIBS® game!

SATYR PLAY

NOUN _____

ADJECTIVE _____

PERSON IN ROOM (MALE) _____

VERB _____

PLURAL NOUN _____

TYPE OF FOOD _____

NOUN _____

VERB ENDING IN "ING" _____

VERB _____

VERB ENDING IN "ING" _____

ANIMAL _____

SILLY WORD _____

VERB _____

VERB _____

EXCLAMATION _____

VERB ENDING IN "ING" _____

ADJECTIVE _____

MAD LIBS®
SATYR PLAY

First Satyr: OMG, I'm so bored.

Second Satyr: Me too. Let's play a/an _____ on someone!
NOUN

First Satyr: That's a/an _____ idea! But who?
ADJECTIVE

Second Satyr: How about _____? He's dumb enough to
PERSON IN ROOM (MALE)

_____ for anything.
VERB
(The two _____ hide under a/an _____ tree, waiting for
PLURAL NOUN   TYPE OF FOOD

their _____ to pass by.)
NOUN

First Satyr: Why is he _____ so slow?
VERB ENDING IN "ING"

Second Satyr: I'm so bored I could _____.
VERB

First Satyr: Wait! He's _____ back around.
VERB ENDING IN "ING"

(Second Satyr makes _____ sounds.)
ANIMAL

First Satyr: What are you doing, _____? He'll _____ you!
SILLY WORD   VERB

Second Satyr: I know! Maybe he'll _____ this way.
VERB

First Satyr: _____! You totally scared him. Look, he's
EXCLAMATION

_____ away.
VERB ENDING IN "ING"

Second Satyr: Now we're going to be even *more* _____.
ADJECTIVE

From UNICORNS, MERMAIDS, AND MAD LIBS® • Copyright © 2016 by Penguin Random House LLC.

MAD LIBS® is fun to play with friends, but you can also play it by yourself! To begin with, DO NOT look at the story on the page below. Fill in the blanks on this page with the words called for. Then, using the words you have selected, fill in the blank spaces in the story.

Now you've created your own hilarious MAD LIBS® game!

WITNESS INTERVIEW

ANIMAL _____

VERB _____

A PLACE _____

NUMBER _____

PLURAL NOUN _____

PLURAL NOUN _____

NOUN _____

ANIMAL _____

VERB ENDING IN "ING" _____

ARTICLE OF CLOTHING _____

ADJECTIVE _____

ADVERB _____

EXCLAMATION _____

ADJECTIVE _____

PART OF THE BODY (PLURAL) _____

COLOR _____

VERB _____

Kid: I'm telling you, my sister is a were-_____!
ANIMAL

Officer: Slow down! _____ at the beginning.
VERB

Kid: I got home from (the) _____ _____ hours after my curfew.
A PLACE   NUMBER

I tiptoed upstairs without my _____ noticing. That's when I heard
PLURAL NOUN

_____ coming from my sister's _____-room!
PLURAL NOUN   NOUN

Officer: What did you think was happening?

Kid: At first I thought there was a/an _____ in the room with her. Then
ANIMAL

I heard _____ sounds, like someone or something was ripping
VERB ENDING IN "ING"

her _____ apart. I asked her if she was _____, and
ARTICLE OF CLOTHING   ADJECTIVE

when she didn't answer, I knocked as _____ as I could.
ADVERB

Officer: According to your dad, you screamed, "_____!" Why
EXCLAMATION

didn't you call for help?

Kid: The door opened, and that's when I saw her! She had _____ claws,
ADJECTIVE

and whiskers had grown out of her _____. She looked at me
PART OF THE BODY (PLURAL)

with _____ eyes, and growled, "_____ your own business, twerp!"
COLOR   VERB

MAD LIBS® is fun to play with friends, but you can also play it by yourself! To begin with, DO NOT look at the story on the page below. Fill in the blanks on this page with the words called for. Then, using the words you have selected, fill in the blank spaces in the story.

Now you've created your own hilarious MAD LIBS® game!

RIDDLE OF THE SPHINX

_____
A PLACE

_____
NOUN

_____
ANIMAL

_____
VERB (PAST TENSE)

_____
VERB ENDING IN "S"

_____
PART OF THE BODY (PLURAL)

_____
NUMBER

_____
NOUN

_____
FIRST NAME (MALE)

_____
NOUN

_____
VERB

_____
VERB ENDING IN "S"

_____
ADJECTIVE

_____
NOUN

_____
ADJECTIVE

_____
NOUN

_____
OCCUPATION

According to legends of (the) _____, the Sphinx had the

                                                      A PLACE

_____ of a human and the body of a/an _____. She killed
   NOUN   ANIMAL

and _____ any travelers who couldn't answer
         VERB (PAST TENSE)

the following question: "What creature _____ on four
                               VERB ENDING IN "S"

_____ in the morning, _____ legs at noon, and three
PART OF THE BODY (PLURAL)   NUMBER

in the _____?" Only the hero _____ gave the correct
     NOUN   FIRST NAME (MALE)

answer, leading to the Sphinx's _____. "Man," he said. "Because a
                        NOUN

baby has to _____ before he can walk. Then he _____
         VERB   VERB ENDING IN "S"

on two legs until he's _____. At which point, he uses a/an
                 ADJECTIVE

_____ to keep his balance." The Sphinx was so _____ that
  NOUN   ADJECTIVE

her riddle had been solved that she threw herself off a high _____ and
                                        NOUN

died. Talk about a drama _____!
                OCCUPATION

MAD LIBS® is fun to play with friends, but you can also play it by yourself! To begin with, DO NOT look at the story on the page below. Fill in the blanks on this page with the words called for. Then, using the words you have selected, fill in the blank spaces in the story.

Now you've created your own hilarious MAD LIBS® game!

HOW TO RIDE A UNICORN

NOUN _____

ADVERB _____

VERB _____

ADJECTIVE _____

TYPE OF FOOD _____

ADJECTIVE _____

PART OF THE BODY (PLURAL) _____

NOUN _____

SILLY WORD _____

VERB ENDING IN "ING" _____

PART OF THE BODY _____

SAME PART OF THE BODY _____

ADJECTIVE _____

VERB _____

TYPE OF LIQUID _____

VERB _____

MAD LIBS®
HOW TO RIDE A UNICORN

Dos:

- Unicorns don't have _____-belts, so it's important to hold on
  <small>NOUN</small>

  _____ at all times.
  <small>ADVERB</small>

- Because they can _____ your mind, it's crucial to think only
  <small>VERB</small>

  _____ thoughts while riding a uni-_____.
  <small>ADJECTIVE</small>   <small>TYPE OF FOOD</small>

- If touching a unicorn's _____ horn becomes necessary, be sure
  <small>ADJECTIVE</small>

  to warm up your _____first. (They are quite sensitive
  <small>PART OF THE BODY (PLURAL)</small>

  to changes in _____.)
  <small>NOUN</small>

Don'ts:

- Don't say "yeehaw" or "_____." The unicorn will think you're
  <small>SILLY WORD</small>

  _____ fun of it.
  <small>VERB ENDING IN "ING"</small>

- Never stand _____ to _____ with a unicorn for
  <small>PART OF THE BODY</small> <small>SAME PART OF THE BODY</small>

  too long (for _____ reasons).
  <small>ADJECTIVE</small>

- Whatever you do, never, ever _____ unicorn
  <small>VERB</small>

  _____! It is deadly to the touch and will _____
  <small>TYPE OF LIQUID</small>   <small>VERB</small>

  you for sure. Happy riding!

MAD LIBS® is fun to play with friends, but you can also play it by yourself! To begin with, DO NOT look at the story on the page below. Fill in the blanks on this page with the words called for. Then, using the words you have selected, fill in the blank spaces in the story.

Now you've created your own hilarious MAD LIBS® game!

CENTAUR WRESTLING

_____ ADJECTIVE

_____ COLOR

_____ SILLY WORD

_____ ANIMAL

_____ VERB

_____ NOUN

_____ CELEBRITY (MALE)

_____ COLOR

_____ VERB ENDING IN "ING"

_____ NOUN

_____ PLURAL NOUN

_____ OCCUPATION (PLURAL)

_____ PART OF THE BODY

_____ NUMBER

_____ PLURAL NOUN

_____ VERB ENDING IN "ING"

_____ NOUN

The crowd goes _____ as the _____ Whiz and _____
          ADJECTIVE   COLOR   SILLY WORD

Joe enter the ring. Each of these twin centaurs is half Appaloosa _____
        ANIMAL

and half man. They are favored to _____ tonight at the match in
        VERB

_____ City. Entering the ring behind them is _____'s
  NOUN   CELEBRITY (MALE)

dream duo, the _____ Stallions. The crowd makes _____
       COLOR   VERB ENDING IN "ING"

sounds at the hated visiting team. Following the sound of a/an

_____-shot, all four heavy-weight _____ gallop against
  NOUN   PLURAL NOUN

one another. The Stallions have arms like human _____, which
                          OCCUPATION (PLURAL)

they use to put both their opponents in instant _____-locks. The
                        PART OF THE BODY

referee counts all the way to _____ before the Whiz and Joe break free.
             NUMBER

Against all _____, the hometown heroes manage to dominate the
      PLURAL NOUN

Stallions, _____ them to the mat for the full count. The referee
     VERB ENDING IN "ING"

calls it. The Stallions have lost. The _____ goes wild!
                     NOUN

MAD LIBS® is fun to play with friends, but you can also play it by yourself! To begin with, DO NOT look at the story on the page below. Fill in the blanks on this page with the words called for. Then, using the words you have selected, fill in the blank spaces in the story.

Now you've created your own hilarious MAD LIBS® game!

INTERVIEW WITH A BANSHEE

_____
FIRST NAME (FEMALE)

_____
A PLACE

_____
VERB

_____
PART OF THE BODY (PLURAL)

_____
NOUN

_____
NOUN

_____
VERB

_____
ANIMAL (PLURAL)

_____
ADJECTIVE

_____
VERB ENDING IN "ING"

_____
NUMBER

_____
ADJECTIVE

_____
PLURAL NOUN

_____
NOUN

_____
NOUN

MAD LIBS®
INTERVIEW WITH
A BANSHEE

News Anchor: I'm here with _____, a real-life banshee who
FIRST NAME (FEMALE)

has agreed to talk to us about what it's like living as a monster in (the)

_____.
A PLACE

Banshee: Everyone expects me to _____ all the time, at the top of my
VERB

_____, but I'm actually a fairly quiet person.
PART OF THE BODY (PLURAL)

News Anchor: So you're a/an _____ that doesn't scream?
NOUN

Banshee: I scream as loudly as the next _____. But only when
NOUN

someone is about to _____. A kind of death call. And my neighbors
VERB

aren't exactly dropping like _____.
ANIMAL (PLURAL)

News Anchor: So you don't pose a/an _____ threat to the community
ADJECTIVE

here?

Banshee: Of course not! If anything, I'd be an asset to the

Neighborhood Watch because I can sense danger _____ from
VERB ENDING IN "ING"

_____ miles away.
NUMBER

News Anchor: I feel more _____ already! You heard it here first,
ADJECTIVE

_____ and gentlemen. Banshees mean no _____, so give
PLURAL NOUN NOUN

them all a/an _____, why don't you?
NOUN

MAD LIBS® is fun to play with friends, but you can also play it by yourself! To begin with, DO NOT look at the story on the page below. Fill in the blanks on this page with the words called for. Then, using the words you have selected, fill in the blank spaces in the story.

Now you've created your own hilarious MAD LIBS® game!

MONSTER BONES

PERSON IN ROOM (FEMALE) _____

OCCUPATION _____

NOUN _____

A PLACE _____

NUMBER _____

PLURAL NOUN _____

PLURAL NOUN _____

NUMBER _____

ADJECTIVE _____

VERB (PAST TENSE) _____

ANIMAL _____

ADJECTIVE _____

ADJECTIVE _____

NOUN _____

PART OF THE BODY _____

NOUN _____

ADJECTIVE _____

PLURAL NOUN _____

Dr. _____, the world's leading crypto-_____,
   PERSON IN ROOM (FEMALE)   OCCUPATION

asserts that there isn't a/an _____ of proof that the fabled Cyclops ever
                             NOUN

existed in (the) _____. "For more than _____ years," she said,
             A PLACE   NUMBER

"_____ have brought me what they were certain were
   PLURAL NOUN

_____ belonging to the _____-eyed beasts. But they were all
  PLURAL NOUN   NUMBER

_____. What they had _____ were in fact ordinary
  ADJECTIVE   VERB (PAST TENSE)

_____ skulls! It was a/an _____ enough mistake considering
  ANIMAL   ADJECTIVE

that each had a/an _____ hole at the center where the living animal's
             ADJECTIVE

_____ would be, the same size and position as a Cyclops's
  NOUN

_____ socket." The scholar wants nothing more than to put the
 PART OF THE BODY

_____ to rest, once and for all. "I have _____ work to do!"
  NOUN   ADJECTIVE

she says. "I can't spend all day teaching elephant anatomy to _____."
                                                    PLURAL NOUN

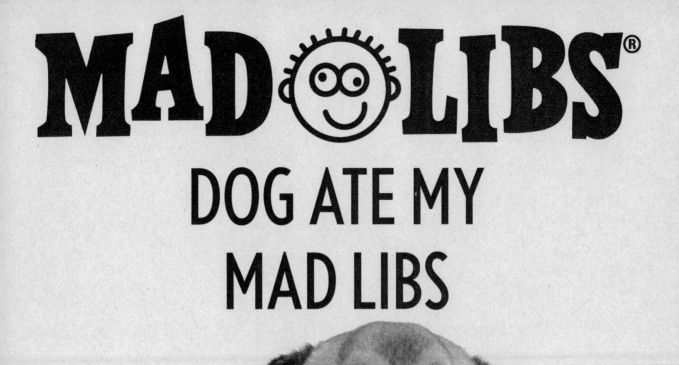

DOG ATE MY
MAD LIBS

by Leigh Olsen

Mad Libs
An Imprint of Penguin Random House

INSTRUCTIONS

MAD LIBS® is a game for people who don't like games!
It can be played by one, two, three, four, or forty.

• RIDICULOUSLY SIMPLE DIRECTIONS

In this tablet you will find stories containing blank spaces where words are left out. One player, the READER, selects one of these stories. The READER does not tell anyone what the story is about. Instead, he/she asks the other players, the WRITERS, to give him/her words. These words are used to fill in the blank spaces in the story.

• TO PLAY

The READER asks each WRITER in turn to call out a word—an adjective or a noun or whatever the space calls for—and uses them to fill in the blank spaces in the story. The result is a MAD LIBS® game.

When the READER then reads the completed MAD LIBS® game to the other players, they will discover that they have written a story that is fantastic, screamingly funny, shocking, silly, crazy, or just plain dumb—depending upon which words each WRITER called out.

• EXAMPLE (*Before* and *After*)

"_____!" he said _____
       EXCLAMATION   ADVERB

as he jumped into his convertible _____ and
                                              NOUN

drove off with his _____ wife.
                        ADJECTIVE

"_____**OUCH**_____!" he said _____**STUPIDLY**_____
       EXCLAMATION   ADVERB

as he jumped into his convertible _____**CAT**_____ and
                                              NOUN

drove off with his _____**BRAVE**_____ wife.
                        ADJECTIVE

MAD LIBS®

QUICK REVIEW

In case you have forgotten what adjectives, adverbs, nouns, and verbs are, here is a quick review:

An ADJECTIVE describes something or somebody. *Lumpy, soft, ugly, messy,* and *short* are adjectives.

An ADVERB tells how something is done. It modifies a verb and usually ends in "ly." *Modestly, stupidly, greedily,* and *carefully* are adverbs.

A NOUN is the name of a person, place, or thing. *Sidewalk, umbrella, bridle, bathtub,* and *nose* are nouns.

A VERB is an action word. *Run, pitch, jump,* and *swim* are verbs. Put the verbs in past tense if the directions say PAST TENSE. *Ran, pitched, jumped,* and *swam* are verbs in the past tense.

When we ask for A PLACE, we mean any sort of place: a country or city *(Spain, Cleveland)* or a room *(bathroom, kitchen).*

An EXCLAMATION or SILLY WORD is any sort of funny sound, gasp, grunt, or outcry, like *Wow!, Ouch!, Whomp!, Ick!,* and *Gadzooks!*

When we ask for specific words, like a NUMBER, a COLOR, an ANIMAL, or a PART OF THE BODY, we mean a word that is one of those things, like *seven, blue, horse,* or *head.*

When we ask for a PLURAL, it means more than one. For example, *cat* pluralized is *cats.*

MAD LIBS® is fun to play with friends, but you can also play it by yourself! To begin with, DO NOT look at the story on the page below. Fill in the blanks on this page with the words called for. Then, using the words you have selected, fill in the blank spaces in the story.

Now you've created your own hilarious MAD LIBS® game!

DOG DAYS

VERB ENDING IN "ING" _____

PART OF THE BODY _____

PLURAL NOUN _____

VERB _____

NOUN _____

A PLACE _____

ADVERB _____

NOUN _____

PLURAL NOUN _____

PART OF THE BODY _____

PART OF THE BODY _____

PLURAL NOUN _____

PLURAL NOUN _____

NOUN _____

MAD LIBS®
DOG DAYS

Have you always wondered what it's like to be a dog?

7:00 a.m.: I wake up and my tummy is _____.
                                          VERB ENDING IN "ING"
I bug my human

by licking her _____ until I get a bowl of _____.
              PART OF THE BODY   PLURAL NOUN

7:30 a.m.: Potty time! My human takes me outside to _____ on a/an
                                                     VERB

_____.
NOUN

8:00 a.m.: My human leaves to go to (the) _____. I am sad and pout
                                          A PLACE

_____.
ADVERB

9:00 a.m.: Naptime. I cuddle on my favorite _____ and dream about
                                            NOUN

chasing _____.
        PLURAL NOUN

6:00 p.m.: MY HUMAN IS HOME! FINALLY! I wag my _____
                                               PART OF THE BODY

back and forth, and give my human kisses on the _____.
                                                PART OF THE BODY

6:30 p.m.: My human takes me for a walk, and I sniff lots of _____.
                                                            PLURAL NOUN

7:00 p.m.: Dinnertime! Eating _____ is my favorite!
                             PLURAL NOUN

9:00 p.m.: I snuggle up next to my human and fall asleep, happy as

a/an _____.
     NOUN

MAD LIBS® is fun to play with friends, but you can also play it by yourself! To begin with, DO NOT look at the story on the page below. Fill in the blanks on this page with the words called for. Then, using the words you have selected, fill in the blank spaces in the story.

Now you've created your own hilarious MAD LIBS® game!

WHO'S THAT DOG?, PART 1

A PLACE _____

NOUN _____

PLURAL NOUN _____

VERB _____

VERB ENDING IN "ING" _____

ADJECTIVE _____

ADJECTIVE _____

ADJECTIVE _____

NOUN _____

ADJECTIVE _____

ADJECTIVE _____

VERB _____

A PLACE _____

NOUN _____

With hundreds of breeds of dogs in (the) _____, there's one for every
                                        A PLACE

kind of _____. Here are a few popular breeds:
          NOUN

Golden retriever: The golden retriever is one of the most popular family

_____. Intelligent and eager to _____, the golden retriever
PLURAL NOUN   VERB

makes an excellent _____ companion, and is also a/an
                    VERB ENDING IN "ING"

_____ guide dog.
ADJECTIVE

Pug: The pug is a lot of dog in a very _____ package. It is known
                                           ADJECTIVE

for being loving, outgoing, and _____. And it snores like a freight
                                ADJECTIVE

_____!
NOUN

Siberian husky: The husky was bred to pull _____ sleds, and it is
                                                ADJECTIVE

known for its _____ endurance and willingness to _____.
              ADJECTIVE   VERB

German shepherd: The German shepherd is not only the most popular police,

guard, and military dog in (the) _____, it is also a loving family
                                 A PLACE

_____.
NOUN

MAD LIBS® is fun to play with friends, but you can also play it by yourself! To begin with, DO NOT look at the story on the page below. Fill in the blanks on this page with the words called for. Then, using the words you have selected, fill in the blank spaces in the story.

Now you've created your own hilarious MAD LIBS® game!

FAMOUS FIDOS: RIN TIN TIN

_____ NOUN

_____ PERSON IN ROOM

_____ A PLACE

_____ VERB

_____ CELEBRITY

_____ PERSON IN ROOM

_____ ADJECTIVE

_____ A PLACE

_____ NOUN

_____ NOUN

_____ ADJECTIVE

_____ PLURAL NOUN

_____ NOUN

MAD LIBS®
FAMOUS FIDOS: RIN TIN TIN

Rin Tin Tin was the biggest movie-star pooch to ever grace the silver

_____. During World War I, Rin Tin Tin's owner and future

NOUN

trainer, _____, discovered the German shepherd puppy on a war-

PERSON IN ROOM

torn battlefield in (the) _____. He brought Rin Tin Tin back

A PLACE

to the United States, trained him to _____, and brought him to

VERB

Hollywood, home to celebrities like _____ and _____.

CELEBRITY   PERSON IN ROOM

Soon, Rin Tin Tin began to receive _____ roles in silent films!

ADJECTIVE

He quickly became one of the most famous stars in (the) _____.

A PLACE

In 1929, Rin Tin Tin even received the most votes for the Academy Award

for Best _____—but the Academy decided to give the award to

NOUN

a/an _____ instead. All in all, this _____ dog starred in

NOUN   ADJECTIVE

twenty-seven major motion _____. He even has his own star on the

PLURAL NOUN

Hollywood Walk of _____!

NOUN

MAD LIBS® is fun to play with friends, but you can also play it by yourself! To begin with, DO NOT look at the story on the page below. Fill in the blanks on this page with the words called for. Then, using the words you have selected, fill in the blank spaces in the story.

Now you've created your own hilarious MAD LIBS® game!

ODE TO THE MUTT

ADJECTIVE _____

PART OF THE BODY _____

PLURAL NOUN _____

PLURAL NOUN _____

PLURAL NOUN _____

NOUN _____

PART OF THE BODY _____

NOUN _____

NOUN _____

A PLACE _____

ANIMAL _____

ADJECTIVE _____

MAD LIBS®
ODE TO THE MUTT

A little bit of this and a little bit of that, the mutt is a/an _____
ADJECTIVE
mixed-breed pup that will warm your _____ and chase your
PART OF THE BODY
_____ away. First of all, mutts are just like snowflakes—no two
PLURAL NOUN
_____ are alike! Mutts come in all shapes and _____.
PLURAL NOUN   PLURAL NOUN
Big ones, small ones, fluffy ones, and scruffy ones—there's a mutt for every

_____. Mutts have a special way of worming their way into your
NOUN

_____. There are millions in shelters that need your love and
PART OF THE BODY

_____. They need your love more than the average _____,
NOUN   NOUN
and they'll love you to (the) _____ and back! So next time you are
A PLACE
thinking about bringing home a new _____, consider adopting a/an
ANIMAL
_____ mutt!
ADJECTIVE

MAD LIBS® is fun to play with friends, but you can also play it by yourself! To begin with, DO NOT look at the story on the page below. Fill in the blanks on this page with the words called for. Then, using the words you have selected, fill in the blank spaces in the story.

Now you've created your own hilarious MAD LIBS® game!

BEGGING 101

NOUN _____

ADJECTIVE _____

PLURAL NOUN _____

NOUN _____

NOUN _____

PART OF THE BODY (PLURAL) _____

ADJECTIVE _____

PART OF THE BODY (PLURAL) _____

ADVERB _____

ADJECTIVE _____

NOUN _____

TYPE OF FOOD _____

PERSON IN ROOM _____

Are your humans cooking a delicious-smelling _____? Learn to
NOUN

beg like a pro with these _____ tips, and you'll be eating tasty
ADJECTIVE

_____ in no time!
PLURAL NOUN

- Identify the weakest _____ at the dinner table. Who is the most likely
NOUN

  to sneak you a/an _____? Sit as close to that person as possible.
NOUN

- Stare up at your target with your biggest, saddest puppy-dog
  _____. If possible, think of something that makes you
PART OF THE BODY (PLURAL)

  feel _____ so you can work up some tears.
ADJECTIVE

- Squint your _____ so you look extra weak and hungry.
PART OF THE BODY (PLURAL)

  Lie down on the ground and pout _____. Basically, make yourself
ADVERB

  look as pathetic and _____ as possible.
ADJECTIVE

- Still not getting any food? Try crying like a/an _____.
NOUN

- If all else fails, grab that delicious _____ with your teeth and
TYPE OF FOOD

  make a run for it—quick! Before _____ catches you!
PERSON IN ROOM

DOGGY DREAMS

———————————— ADJECTIVE

———————————— PART OF THE BODY (PLURAL)

———————————— ADVERB

———————————— ADJECTIVE

———————————— EXCLAMATION

———————————— VERB ENDING IN "ING"

———————————— NOUN

———————————— PART OF THE BODY (PLURAL)

———————————— EXCLAMATION

———————————— NOUN

———————————— SAME NOUN

———————————— PLURAL NOUN

———————————— VERB

———————————— PART OF THE BODY (PLURAL)

———————————— PLURAL NOUN

———————————— PERSON IN ROOM

———————————— PART OF THE BODY

———————————— ADJECTIVE

MAD LIBS
DOGGY DREAMS

You know what it looks like when your sleeping dog is having a/an _____
ADJECTIVE

dream: Their tail swishes, their _____ twitch, and they
PART OF THE BODY (PLURAL)

bark _____. But what do dogs dream about? Here's one dog's
ADVERB

_____ dream:
ADJECTIVE

_____! What's that little flash of white fur _____
EXCLAMATION   VERB ENDING IN "ING"

in my backyard? It's a bunny _____! I have to chase it! I run, run,
NOUN

run, as fast my _____ will carry me. Oh, _____!
PART OF THE BODY (PLURAL)   EXCLAMATION

The bunny has hidden in a/an _____! I sniff the _____,
NOUN   SAME NOUN

and sure enough, it's in there with a den of baby _____! I want
PLURAL NOUN

to play with them so bad, I could _____! I bark at the top of my
VERB

_____. Come out and play, you fluffy little _____!
PART OF THE BODY (PLURAL)   PLURAL NOUN

But before I can, _____ scratches my _____ and wakes
PERSON IN ROOM   PART OF THE BODY

me up. It was all just a/an _____ dream!
ADJECTIVE

MAD LIBS® is fun to play with friends, but you can also play it by yourself! To begin with, DO NOT look at the story on the page below. Fill in the blanks on this page with the words called for. Then, using the words you have selected, fill in the blank spaces in the story.

Now you've created your own hilarious MAD LIBS® game!

WHO'S THAT DOG?, PART 2

_____ ADJECTIVE

_____ VERB

_____ ADJECTIVE

_____ ADJECTIVE

_____ PART OF THE BODY (PLURAL)

_____ ADJECTIVE

_____ ADJECTIVE

_____ PLURAL NOUN

_____ ADJECTIVE

_____ PLURAL NOUN

_____ NOUN

_____ NOUN

MAD LIBS
WHO'S THAT DOG?, PART 2

More _____ dog breeds for you to love and _____!
                ADJECTIVE   VERB

Poodle: The curly-haired poodle, best known for its _____ haircut,
                                                          ADJECTIVE

is exceptionally smart and _____.
                            ADJECTIVE

Dachshund: Known for its long body and short _____,
                                                  PART OF THE BODY (PLURAL)

the dachshund has a friendly personality and a/an _____ sense of
                                                    ADJECTIVE

smell.

Beagle: This hunting dog is happy-go-_____, friendly, and loves
                                          ADJECTIVE

the company of humans and other _____.
                                 PLURAL NOUN

Great Dane: The gentle Great Dane, famous for its _____ size, is
                                                       ADJECTIVE

also known as "the king of _____."
                            PLURAL NOUN

Chihuahua: This sassy little _____, often called a "purse dog," is a
                                  NOUN

big dog in a little _____.
                     NOUN

MAD LIBS® is fun to play with friends, but you can also play it by yourself! To begin with, DO NOT look at the story on the page below. Fill in the blanks on this page with the words called for. Then, using the words you have selected, fill in the blank spaces in the story.

Now you've created your own hilarious MAD LIBS® game!

FAMOUS FIDOS: LASSIE

ADJECTIVE _____

ADJECTIVE _____

A PLACE _____

PERSON IN ROOM (MALE) _____

ADJECTIVE _____

ADJECTIVE _____

VERB _____

ADVERB _____

PERSON IN ROOM (MALE) _____

NOUN _____

NOUN _____

NOUN _____

ADJECTIVE _____

NOUN _____

FAMOUS FIDOS: LASSIE

Lassie the collie was famous for her heroics on television and the

_____ screen. On the TV show _Lassie_, the collie lived in
  ADJECTIVE

a/an _____ farming community in (the) _____. Lassie
     ADJECTIVE   A PLACE

belonged to an eleven-year-old boy named _____, as well as
                                    PERSON IN ROOM (MALE)

his mother and _____ grandfather. Whenever the _____
           ADJECTIVE   ADJECTIVE

boy got into trouble, Lassie would _____ to the rescue, or she would
                            VERB

run and find help. "BARK, BARK!" Lassie would say _____.
                                       ADVERB

"What's that, girl?" the person would ask. "Little _____ fell
                                  PERSON IN ROOM (MALE)

down a/an _____?" Quick as a/an _____, the trapped
           NOUN   NOUN

_____ would be safe and _____. And once again, Lassie
   NOUN   ADJECTIVE

saved the _____!
         NOUN

MAD LIBS® is fun to play with friends, but you can also play it by yourself! To begin with, DO NOT look at the story on the page below. Fill in the blanks on this page with the words called for. Then, using the words you have selected, fill in the blank spaces in the story.

Now you've created your own hilarious MAD LIBS® game!

HAIL TO THE POOCH

PERSON IN ROOM _____

ADJECTIVE _____

ADJECTIVE _____

PLURAL NOUN _____

TYPE OF FOOD _____

NOUN _____

ADJECTIVE _____

ADJECTIVE _____

NOUN _____

NOUN _____

CELEBRITY _____

NOUN _____

From George Washington to _____ to Barack Obama, many
                              PERSON IN ROOM

United States presidents have been _____ dog lovers. Here's a list of
                                        ADJECTIVE

_____ First Dogs:
   ADJECTIVE

- **Laddie Boy:** Warren G. Harding once invited neighborhood _____
                                                                PLURAL NOUN

   to the White House for his Airedale terrier's birthday party, where they ate

   _____ made of dog biscuits!
     TYPE OF FOOD

- **Fala:** Franklin Delano Roosevelt's beloved Scottish terrier was

   named after an Army _____ and had his own _____
                             NOUN   ADJECTIVE

   secretary. Fala even starred in a/an _____ movie!
                                            ADJECTIVE

- **Millie:** George H.W. Bush's springer spaniel published her own book,

   ghostwritten by the First _____, which sold more copies than
                                  NOUN

   President Bush's _____!
                        NOUN

- **Bo and Sunny:** Barack Obama received Bo the Portuguese water dog as a

   gift from _____. A few years later, the First Family got Sunny,
                 CELEBRITY

   another Portuguese water _____.
                                 NOUN

MAD LIBS® is fun to play with friends, but you can also play it by yourself! To begin with, DO NOT look at the story on the page below. Fill in the blanks on this page with the words called for. Then, using the words you have selected, fill in the blank spaces in the story.

Now you've created your own hilarious MAD LIBS® game!

CANINE CAREERS

_____ PLURAL NOUN

_____ ADJECTIVE

_____ PART OF THE BODY

_____ A PLACE

_____ A PLACE

_____ ADJECTIVE

_____ PLURAL NOUN

_____ PART OF THE BODY (PLURAL)

_____ PLURAL NOUN

_____ PLURAL NOUN

_____ ADJECTIVE

_____ ADJECTIVE

_____ PART OF THE BODY (PLURAL)

_____ PLURAL NOUN

Not all dogs nap and play with their toy _____ all day. Some dogs
                                        PLURAL NOUN

have _____ jobs!
     ADJECTIVE

- **Guide dogs:** Guide dogs, or Seeing _____ dogs, help lead
                                        PART OF THE BODY

  the blind where they need to go, like to (the) _____ or (the)
                                                 A PLACE

  _____.
   A PLACE

- **Military dogs:** These dogs help troops in _____ military
                                               ADJECTIVE

  missions. They act as guard dogs, looking out for _____, and
                                                    PLURAL NOUN

  they use their powerful _____ to sniff out dangerous
                          PART OF THE BODY (PLURAL)

  _____. US Air Force dogs even jump out of flying _____
   PLURAL NOUN   PLURAL NOUN

  with their airmen!

- **Search-and-rescue dogs:** In a/an _____ disaster or
                                      ADJECTIVE

  in the _____ wilderness, these dogs use their powerful
         ADJECTIVE

  _____ to help track down missing _____.
   PART OF THE BODY (PLURAL)   PLURAL NOUN

MAD LIBS® is fun to play with friends, but you can also play it by yourself! To begin with, DO NOT look at the story on the page below. Fill in the blanks on this page with the words called for. Then, using the words you have selected, fill in the blank spaces in the story.

Now you've created your own hilarious MAD LIBS® game!

DIVA DOG

ADJECTIVE _____

NOUN _____

PART OF THE BODY _____

SILLY WORD _____

SAME SILLY WORD _____

A PLACE _____

NOUN _____

NOUN _____

NOUN _____

PART OF THE BODY _____

ADJECTIVE _____

VERB ENDING IN "S" _____

ADJECTIVE _____

PART OF THE BODY _____

ADJECTIVE _____

NOUN _____

MAD LIBS
DIVA DOG

Who's that _____ pooch with the fluffy little _____
           ADJECTIVE   NOUN

and the cute _____? Why, that's Little Miss _____!
             PART OF THE BODY   SILLY WORD

Little Miss _____ is famous throughout (the) _____.
             SAME SILLY WORD   A PLACE

Her _____ is splashed all over the Internet, and in books and
        NOUN

magazines like _____ *Weekly* and *Life &* _____. Little
            NOUN   NOUN

Miss can't go anywhere without someone recognizing her _____!
                                           PART OF THE BODY

Luckily, Little Miss likes attention from the _____ pup-parazzi. She
                                  ADJECTIVE

_____ for the cameras, and greets all her _____ fans with
VERB ENDING IN "S"   ADJECTIVE

a smile on her _____. After all, without her _____ fans,
          PART OF THE BODY   ADJECTIVE

Little Miss would be just another cute face in the _____!
                                          NOUN

WHO'S THAT DOG?, PART 3

_____ NOUN

_____ ADJECTIVE

_____ ANIMAL (PLURAL)

_____ NOUN

_____ NOUN

_____ PART OF THE BODY

_____ NOUN

_____ PART OF THE BODY

_____ NOUN

_____ PLURAL NOUN

_____ VERB ENDING IN "ING"

_____ PLURAL NOUN

_____ PART OF THE BODY

_____ NOUN

_____ PLURAL NOUN

A few more dog breeds to brighten your _____!
NOUN

Yorkshire terrier: Yorkies may be small, but they are brave and _____.
ADJECTIVE

Yorkies were originally bred to hunt _____ in _____
ANIMAL (PLURAL)   NOUN

factories!

Doberman pinscher: The Doberman is a muscular _____. With
NOUN

its intelligent _____ , the Doberman is often trained as a police
PART OF THE BODY

_____.
NOUN

Shih tzu: The shih tzu has a long and luxurious _____. This
PART OF THE BODY

playful _____ is usually friendly toward all _____.
NOUN   PLURAL NOUN

Australian shepherd: Aussies are very energetic and require daily

_____ to be happy. They are great at herding crowds of
VERB ENDING IN "ING"

_____ on the farm.
PLURAL NOUN

Pomeranian: The Pomeranian has a big, fluffy _____ to match
PART OF THE BODY

its outgoing _____. This intelligent little dog loves to please its
NOUN

_____.
PLURAL NOUN

MAD LIBS® is fun to play with friends, but you can also play it by yourself! To begin with, DO NOT look at the story on the page below. Fill in the blanks on this page with the words called for. Then, using the words you have selected, fill in the blank spaces in the story.

Now you've created your own hilarious MAD LIBS® game!

POOCH PALACE

ADJECTIVE _____

ANIMAL _____

NOUN _____

TYPE OF LIQUID _____

ADJECTIVE _____

PART OF THE BODY _____

OCCUPATION _____

NOUN _____

SILLY WORD _____

PART OF THE BODY _____

A PLACE _____

PART OF THE BODY _____

NOUN _____

PLURAL NOUN _____

MAD LIBS®
POOCH PALACE

Welcome to the _____ Pooch Palace, the dog spa for all your
                        ADJECTIVE

grooming needs! Below is our spa menu. How do you want to pamper your

_____ today?
    ANIMAL

- **Paw-dicure:** We'll not only trim your _____'s nails, we'll paint
                                              NOUN

  them with a coat of _____ so your pup looks _____
                  TYPE OF LIQUID   ADJECTIVE

  and stylish.

- **Pup massage:** If your dog is in need of some rest and relaxation,

  a/an _____ massage might be just what the _____
        PART OF THE BODY   OCCUPATION

  ordered!

- **Doggy 'do:** Is your _____ looking shaggy? Our renowned stylist,
                          NOUN

  Pierre _____, gives the best _____-cut this side of
          SILLY WORD   PART OF THE BODY

  (the) _____.
        A PLACE

- **Fur dye:** If you've ever wanted your dog's _____ to match the
                                         PART OF THE BODY

  color of your favorite _____, look no further. The Pooch Palace
                          NOUN

  will make all your _____ come true!
              PLURAL NOUN

MAD LIBS® is fun to play with friends, but you can also play it by yourself! To begin with, DO NOT look at the story on the page below. Fill in the blanks on this page with the words called for. Then, using the words you have selected, fill in the blank spaces in the story.

Now you've created your own hilarious MAD LIBS® game!

HOMEWARD BOUND

A PLACE _____

ADJECTIVE _____

PERSON IN ROOM (FEMALE) _____

NUMBER _____

VERB (PAST TENSE) _____

PERSON IN ROOM _____

PART OF THE BODY (PLURAL) _____

NOUN _____

ADJECTIVE _____

NOUN _____

NOUN _____

PERSON IN ROOM _____

TYPE OF LIQUID _____

ADJECTIVE _____

MAD LIBS®
HOMEWARD BOUND

In (the) _____ today, one _____ family was reunited with
     A PLACE   ADJECTIVE

their beloved dog, _____, who made her way home after
           PERSON IN ROOM (FEMALE)

being missing for _____ days. "She just showed up on our front
               NUMBER

doorstep this morning and _____," said _____. "We
              VERB (PAST TENSE)   PERSON IN ROOM

couldn't believe our _____." The family dog disappeared
           PART OF THE BODY (PLURAL)

after leaving the family's front yard to chase after a wild _____ one
                                         NOUN

afternoon, and the family has been worried _____ ever since. They
                              ADJECTIVE

put up "lost _____" posters all over the neighborhood, and even
            NOUN

put a/an _____ in the local newspaper. "We have no idea where
           NOUN

she's been all this time," said _____. "We're just happier than
                     PERSON IN ROOM

a pig in _____ that she's home again. We can't wait to spoil her
        TYPE OF LIQUID

_____."
  ADJECTIVE

MAD LIBS® is fun to play with friends, but you can also play it by yourself! To begin with, DO NOT look at the story on the page below. Fill in the blanks on this page with the words called for. Then, using the words you have selected, fill in the blank spaces in the story.

Now you've created your own hilarious MAD LIBS® game!

WONDER DOG

_____ VERB

_____ ADJECTIVE

_____ PART OF THE BODY (PLURAL)

_____ ADJECTIVE

_____ NOUN

_____ PART OF THE BODY

_____ VERB ENDING IN "ING"

_____ ADJECTIVE

_____ PART OF THE BODY (PLURAL)

_____ ADVERB

_____ NOUN

_____ ADJECTIVE

_____ PLURAL NOUN

_____ ADJECTIVE

_____ ADJECTIVE

_____ ADVERB

_____ VERB

MAD LIBS®
WONDER DOG

Lots of dogs can sit, stay, and _____. But not many can do these

_____ tricks!
ADJECTIVE

- **Play dead:** When you say, "Bang! Bang!" some dogs will roll onto their

_____ and act _____. This act is sure to
PART OF THE BODY (PLURAL)   ADJECTIVE

tickle your funny _____.
NOUN

- **Dance:** Your dog may know how to wag its _____ to the beat,
PART OF THE BODY

but can it dance like nobody's _____? A dog that knows
VERB ENDING IN "ING"

this _____ trick can stand on its hind _____
ADJECTIVE   PART OF THE BODY (PLURAL)

and spin around _____!
ADVERB

- **Bring my slippers:** Feeling lazy and don't want to get out of your

comfy _____? Ask your dog to do it! If your dog knows this
NOUN

_____ trick, say, "Bring my slippers," and your dog will bring
ADJECTIVE

your _____ to you!
PLURAL NOUN

- **Jump rope:** If your dog knows this _____ trick, grab a/an
ADJECTIVE

_____ rope and a partner, swing the rope _____, and
ADJECTIVE   ADVERB

your dog will _____ over it again and again!
VERB

MAD LIBS® is fun to play with friends, but you can also play it by yourself! To begin with, DO NOT look at the story on the page below. Fill in the blanks on this page with the words called for. Then, using the words you have selected, fill in the blank spaces in the story.

Now you've created your own hilarious MAD LIBS® game!

DOG'S DELIGHT

_____ VERB ENDING IN "S"

_____ PART OF THE BODY

_____ ADJECTIVE

_____ PLURAL NOUN

_____ ANIMAL

_____ VERB

_____ VERB

_____ PLURAL NOUN

_____ NOUN

_____ PLURAL NOUN

_____ NOUN

_____ NOUN

_____ NOUN

_____ PLURAL NOUN

_____ NOUN

_____ ADJECTIVE

_____ PART OF THE BODY

_____ NOUN

You know your dog is happy when it _____ and wags its
$\qquad$ VERB ENDING IN "S"

_____ back and forth. If you want your dog to be _____
PART OF THE BODY $\qquad$ ADJECTIVE

as a clam at all times, try any of the following _____. It's a countdown
$\qquad$ PLURAL NOUN

of your _____ 's favorite things!
$\qquad$ ANIMAL

5. **Walks:** Though some dogs would rather stay home and _____,
$\qquad$ VERB

most dogs love to go for walks to _____ on fire hydrants and sniff
$\qquad$ VERB

_____.
PLURAL NOUN

4. **Naps:** Dogs love to curl up on a/an _____ and dream about
$\qquad$ NOUN

_____—especially if they're cuddling with their favorite
PLURAL NOUN

_____.
NOUN

3. **Playtime:** Fidos love to play fetch with a/an _____ or run around
$\qquad$ NOUN

chasing a/an _____. Sometimes, _____ just wanna
$\qquad$ NOUN $\qquad$ PLURAL NOUN

have fun!

2. **Food:** Whether it's a can of dog _____ or _____ table
$\qquad$ NOUN $\qquad$ ADJECTIVE

scraps, dogs love to eat. The way to a dog's heart is definitely through its

_____!
PART OF THE BODY

1. **You!:** After all, a dog is a/an _____ 's best friend.
$\qquad$ NOUN

MAD LIBS® is fun to play with friends, but you can also play it by yourself! To begin with, DO NOT look at the story on the page below. Fill in the blanks on this page with the words called for. Then, using the words you have selected, fill in the blank spaces in the story.

Now you've created your own hilarious MAD LIBS® game!

WHO'S THAT DOG?, PART 4

VERB _____

COLOR _____

NOUN _____

VERB ENDING IN "ING" _____

NOUN _____

PART OF THE BODY _____

VERB _____

PART OF THE BODY (PLURAL) _____

A PLACE _____

NUMBER _____

ADJECTIVE _____

VERB _____

ADJECTIVE _____

PLURAL NOUN _____

A PLACE _____

ADJECTIVE _____

MAD LIBS®
WHO'S THAT DOG?, PART 4

A final few furry dog breeds for you to love and _____ :
                                                    VERB

Collie: The brown and _____ collie is a friendly family _____,
                            COLOR   NOUN

known for its grace and elegance when _____.
                                        VERB ENDING IN "ING"

Dalmation: This black-and-white _____ is the only dog breed
                                        NOUN

with spots on its _____. They have lots of energy and need to
                    PART OF THE BODY

_____ a lot.
    VERB

Pembroke Welsh corgi: The corgi is known for its very short

_____ and stout body. The queen of (the) _____
PART OF THE BODY (PLURAL)   A PLACE

owns _____ corgis!
        NUMBER

Miniature schnauzer: The miniature schnauzer may be small, but it is

a/an _____ guard dog, and will _____ at the sign of any
        ADJECTIVE   VERB

_____ intruder.
    ADJECTIVE

St. Bernard: The St. Bernard was originally used to hunt for _____
                                                                    PLURAL NOUN

during snowstorms in (the) _____. They are very gentle and
                              A PLACE

_____.
    ADJECTIVE

MAD LIBS® is fun to play with friends, but you can also play it by yourself! To begin with, DO NOT look at the story on the page below. Fill in the blanks on this page with the words called for. Then, using the words you have selected, fill in the blank spaces in the story.

Now you've created your own hilarious MAD LIBS® game!

LET'S GO FOR A RIDE!

PERSON IN ROOM _____

PART OF THE BODY (PLURAL) _____

PART OF THE BODY (PLURAL) _____

ADJECTIVE _____

NOUN _____

NOUN _____

PART OF THE BODY _____

PLURAL NOUN _____

PART OF THE BODY (PLURAL) _____

PART OF THE BODY _____

ADJECTIVE _____

ADVERB _____

NOUN _____

PERSON IN ROOM _____

EXCLAMATION _____

NOUN _____

MAD LIBS®
LET'S GO FOR A RIDE!

"_____, come!" I hear my owner call out. My _____
PERSON IN ROOM   PART OF THE BODY (PLURAL)

perk up—is that the sound of the garage door opening? Suddenly, I am excited

from my head to my _____. Can it be? Am I going
PART OF THE BODY (PLURAL)

for a/an _____ car ride? I bound to the door, where I see my owner
ADJECTIVE

getting into the car. She pats the seat. "Come on, _____!" she calls.
NOUN

This is the best _____ ever! I hop happily into the front seat and
NOUN

immediately stick my _____ out of the car window. We drive
PART OF THE BODY

away down the street, passing houses and mailboxes and _____.
PLURAL NOUN

I can feel the wind in my _____ and the sun on my
PART OF THE BODY (PLURAL)

_____, and everything smells _____. *Where are we*
PART OF THE BODY   ADJECTIVE

going? I wonder _____. So you can imagine my _____ as
ADVERB   NOUN

we pulled into the parking lot of Dr. _____'s office. *We're going to*
PERSON IN ROOM

the vet? _____! This is the worst _____ ever!
EXCLAMATION   NOUN

FAMOUS FIDOS: SCOOBY-DOO

_____ NOUN

_____ NOUN

_____ PERSON IN ROOM (FEMALE)

_____ PERSON IN ROOM (MALE)

_____ NOUN

_____ ADJECTIVE

_____ PLURAL NOUN

_____ PLURAL NOUN

_____ SAME PLURAL NOUN

_____ PLURAL NOUN

_____ PLURAL NOUN

_____ ADJECTIVE

_____ SILLY WORD

MAD LIBS® is fun to play with friends, but you can also
play it by yourself! To begin with, DO NOT look at the
story on the page below. Fill in the blanks on this page
with the words called for. Then, using the words you
have selected, fill in the blank spaces in the story.

Now you've created your own hilarious MAD LIBS® game!

MAD LIBS
FAMOUS FIDOS: SCOOBY-DOO

Scooby-Doo is the star of the animated television _____ *Scooby-*
NOUN

Doo, Where Are You! Scooby-Doo, also known as Scooby, is a talking

_____ who solves mysteries along with four teenagers named Shaggy,
NOUN

Daphne, _____, and _____. Scooby-
PERSON IN ROOM (FEMALE)   PERSON IN ROOM (MALE)

Doo, a Great _____, belongs to his _____ friend, Shaggy.
NOUN   ADJECTIVE

Much like Shaggy, Scooby is scared of _____ and is always hungry
PLURAL NOUN

for cookies called Scooby _____. Luckily, the prospect of eating
PLURAL NOUN

Scooby _____ and keeping his friends safe from _____
SAME PLURAL NOUN   PLURAL NOUN

helps Scooby to be brave and stand up to scary _____. Scooby and
PLURAL NOUN

his friends always solve the _____ mystery, and Scooby always ends
ADJECTIVE

each episode by saying "_____-dooby-doo!"
SILLY WORD

MAD LIBS® is fun to play with friends, but you can also play it by yourself! To begin with, DO NOT look at the story on the page below. Fill in the blanks on this page with the words called for. Then, using the words you have selected, fill in the blank spaces in the story.

Now you've created your own hilarious MAD LIBS® game!

DOGS VERSUS CATS

_____ ADJECTIVE

_____ ADJECTIVE

_____ PART OF THE BODY

_____ NUMBER

_____ ADJECTIVE

_____ PLURAL NOUN

_____ NOUN

_____ PLURAL NOUN

_____ PART OF THE BODY (PLURAL)

_____ NOUN

_____ PART OF THE BODY

_____ NOUN

_____ NOUN

_____ NOUN

_____ SAME NOUN

_____ ADJECTIVE

_____ NOUN

MAD LIBS®
DOGS VERSUS CATS

Which are better, _____ cats or _____ dogs? Anyone with
             ADJECTIVE   ADJECTIVE

half a/an _____ knows that dogs are _____ times better
       PART OF THE BODY   NUMBER

than cats. Dogs are _____ companions, while cats only care about
               ADJECTIVE

their own _____. Dogs are loyal to their _____, but cats
      PLURAL NOUN   NOUN

will love whoever gives them _____ to eat. Dogs like to have their
                     PLURAL NOUN

_____ rubbed, while cats will bite your _____
PART OF THE BODY (PLURAL)   NOUN

if you try to put a/an _____ on them. Most dogs love going for
            PART OF THE BODY

rides in a/an _____, but cats just get sick all over your favorite
        NOUN

_____. Dogs love to play fetch with a/an _____, but if
  NOUN   NOUN

you throw a/an _____ for a cat, it will just look at you like you're
       SAME NOUN

_____. All in all, when it comes to dogs versus cats, only the dog is
  ADJECTIVE

truly man's best _____.
         NOUN

MAD LIBS® is fun to play with friends, but you can also play it by yourself! To begin with, DO NOT look at the story on the page below. Fill in the blanks on this page with the words called for. Then, using the words you have selected, fill in the blank spaces in the story.

Now you've created your own hilarious MAD LIBS® game!

FOREVER HOME

LAST NAME _____

NOUN _____

ADJECTIVE _____

ADJECTIVE _____

PART OF THE BODY (PLURAL) _____

COLOR _____

PART OF THE BODY _____

ADJECTIVE _____

NOUN _____

A PLACE _____

ADJECTIVE _____

PLURAL NOUN _____

ADJECTIVE _____

ADJECTIVE _____

PART OF THE BODY _____

EXCLAMATION _____

ADVERB _____

MAD LIBS®
FOREVER HOME

When the _____ family went to the animal shelter,
                LAST NAME

they never knew they'd find a/an _____ like Rex. The family
                                    NOUN

looked at all the dogs before making this very _____ decision.
                                                  ADJECTIVE

Sure, the puppies were cute and _____, but one older dog stole the
                                  ADJECTIVE

family's _____. His name was Rex, and with his fuzzy
          PART OF THE BODY (PLURAL)

_____ fur, his crooked _____, and his _____
   COLOR   PART OF THE BODY   ADJECTIVE

personality, the family knew they'd found their new _____. Plus, by
                                                      NOUN

bringing Rex back to (the) _____ with them, they saved his life. Now
                            A PLACE

Rex would have a/an _____ place to sleep, _____ to eat, and
                      ADJECTIVE   PLURAL NOUN

a/an _____ family to call his own. And Rex would more than repay
      ADJECTIVE

his family with lots of _____ wet kisses on the _____
                          ADJECTIVE   PART OF THE BODY

and unconditional love. _____! Rex had found his forever home,
                          EXCLAMATION

and they all lived _____ ever after.
                    ADVERB

MAD LIBS®

ESCAPE FROM DETENTION
MAD LIBS

I will not play Mad Libs in class.
I will not play Mad Libs in class.
I will not play Mad Libs in class.
I will not play Mad Libs in class.
I will not play

by Mickie Matheis

Mad Libs
An Imprint of Penguin Random House

MAD LIBS®

INSTRUCTIONS

MAD LIBS® is a game for people who don't like games!
It can be played by one, two, three, four, or forty.

• RIDICULOUSLY SIMPLE DIRECTIONS

In this tablet you will find stories containing blank spaces where words are left out.
One player, the READER, selects one of these stories. The READER does not tell anyone
what the story is about. Instead, he/she asks the other players, the WRITERS, to give
him/her words. These words are used to fill in the blank spaces in the story.

• TO PLAY

The READER asks each WRITER in turn to call out a word—an adjective or a noun or
whatever the space calls for—and uses them to fill in the blank spaces in the story. The
result is a MAD LIBS® game.

When the READER then reads the completed MAD LIBS® game to the other players,
they will discover that they have written a story that is fantastic, screamingly funny,
shocking, silly, crazy, or just plain dumb—depending upon which words each WRITER
called out.

• EXAMPLE (*Before* and *After*)

"_____!" he said _____
        EXCLAMATION   ADVERB

as he jumped into his convertible _____ and
                                          NOUN

drove off with his _____ wife.
                          ADJECTIVE

"_____OUCH_____!" he said _____STUPIDLY_____
        EXCLAMATION   ADVERB

as he jumped into his convertible _____CAT_____ and
                                          NOUN

drove off with his _____BRAVE_____ wife.
                          ADJECTIVE

MAD LIBS®

QUICK REVIEW

In case you have forgotten what adjectives, adverbs, nouns, and verbs are, here is a quick review:

An ADJECTIVE describes something or somebody. *Lumpy, soft, ugly, messy,* and *short* are adjectives.

An ADVERB tells how something is done. It modifies a verb and usually ends in "ly." *Modestly, stupidly, greedily,* and *carefully* are adverbs.

A NOUN is the name of a person, place, or thing. *Sidewalk, umbrella, bridle, bathtub,* and *nose* are nouns.

A VERB is an action word. *Run, pitch, jump,* and *swim* are verbs. Put the verbs in past tense if the directions say PAST TENSE. *Ran, pitched, jumped,* and *swam* are verbs in the past tense.

When we ask for A PLACE, we mean any sort of place: a country or city *(Spain, Cleveland)* or a room *(bathroom, kitchen).*

An EXCLAMATION or SILLY WORD is any sort of funny sound, gasp, grunt, or outcry, like *Wow!, Ouch!, Whomp!, Ick!,* and *Gadzooks!*

When we ask for specific words, like a NUMBER, a COLOR, an ANIMAL, or a PART OF THE BODY, we mean a word that is one of those things, like *seven, blue, horse,* or *head.*

When we ask for a PLURAL, it means more than one. For example, *cat* pluralized is *cats.*

SENTENCED TO DETENTION
PART 1

_____ A PLACE

_____ PART OF THE BODY

_____ ADJECTIVE

_____ NOUN

_____ PART OF THE BODY

_____ PERSON IN ROOM

_____ NOUN

_____ PLURAL NOUN

_____ ADJECTIVE

_____ TYPE OF LIQUID

_____ PART OF THE BODY

_____ COLOR

_____ NOUN

_____ TYPE OF FOOD

_____ ADJECTIVE

_____ NOUN

_____ ARTICLE OF CLOTHING

_____ NOUN

MAD LIBS®
SENTENCED TO DETENTION
PART 1

Do you want to end up in detention in (the) _____? Be a real pain
                                        A PLACE

in the _____ by engaging in any of these _____
       PART OF THE BODY   _ADJECTIVE_

behaviors:

- Hanging a "Kick Me" _____ on the _____ of
                        NOUN   _PART OF THE BODY_

  _____
  PERSON IN ROOM

- Leaving a sharp _____ on your teacher's chair—*ouch!*
                   NOUN

- Disrupting classes by loudly slamming _____ into the lockers
                                          PLURAL NOUN

- Sneaking a hose into the parking lot and filling the principal's

  _____ car with _____
  ADJECTIVE   _TYPE OF LIQUID_

- Dyeing your _____ neon _____
              PART OF THE BODY   _COLOR_

- Starting a/an _____ fight in the cafeteria—and lobbing
                NOUN

  some creamed _____ at the principal, knocking off his
               TYPE OF FOOD

  _____ hairpiece
  ADJECTIVE

- Jumping up on a/an _____ in the middle of class,
                     NOUN

  ripping open your button-down _____, and yelling, "I'm
                                 ARTICLE OF CLOTHING

  _____-man!"
  NOUN

MAD LIBS® is fun to play with friends, but you can also play it by yourself! To begin with, DO NOT look at the story on the page below. Fill in the blanks on this page with the words called for. Then, using the words you have selected, fill in the blank spaces in the story.

Now you've created your own hilarious MAD LIBS® game!

SENTENCED TO DETENTION
PART 2

_____ ADJECTIVE

_____ NOUN

_____ PERSON IN ROOM

_____ ANIMAL

_____ ADJECTIVE

_____ NOUN

_____ PLURAL NOUN

_____ ADJECTIVE

_____ PART OF THE BODY

_____ VERB ENDING IN "ING"

_____ ADJECTIVE

_____ NOUN

_____ PLURAL NOUN

_____ PART OF THE BODY

_____ TYPE OF LIQUID

_____ ADJECTIVE

Any of these random acts of _____-ness will earn you a one-way

ADJECTIVE

_____ to detention:

NOUN

- Hanging posters with Principal _____'s head on the body

PERSON IN ROOM

  of a/an _____

ANIMAL

- Swearing or saying inappropriate things like, "You big _____

ADJECTIVE

  _____!"

NOUN

- Spray-painting the desks in the classrooms, the _____ in

PLURAL NOUN

  the cafeteria, or other _____ school property

ADJECTIVE

- Coming to class with a tattoo on your _____

PART OF THE BODY

- Talking or _____ with your cell phone during class

VERB ENDING IN "ING"

- Flunking a/an _____ test and then forgetting to have your

ADJECTIVE

  mom or _____ sign it

NOUN

- Littering the floor with crumpled _____

PLURAL NOUN

- Dunking a fellow student's _____ in the _____

PART OF THE BODY   TYPE OF LIQUID

  in the toilet

- Last but not _____, a surefire way to get a detention is to not

ADJECTIVE

  show up for detention!

MAD LIBS® is fun to play with friends, but you can also play it by yourself! To begin with, DO NOT look at the story on the page below. Fill in the blanks on this page with the words called for. Then, using the words you have selected, fill in the blank spaces in the story.

Now you've created your own hilarious MAD LIBS® game!

MY FIRST DETENTION

————————————— PERSON IN ROOM

————————————— LETTER OF THE ALPHABET

————————————— NOUN

————————————— NOUN

————————————— NUMBER

————————————— PLURAL NOUN

————————————— A PLACE

————————————— ADJECTIVE

————————————— ADJECTIVE

————————————— PLURAL NOUN

————————————— TYPE OF FOOD (PLURAL)

————————————— ADVERB

————————————— COLOR

————————————— VERB

————————————— NOUN

————————————— TYPE OF LIQUID

————————————— CELEBRITY (MALE)

————————————— VERB

MAD LIBS®
MY FIRST DETENTION

My name is _____, and today was the worst day of my entire life.

PERSON IN ROOM

Why? I got a detention—my first ever. I don't get detentions! I'm a

straight-_____ student, president of _____

LETTER OF THE ALPHABET   NOUN

Council, and the head of the _____ Club. How was I supposed to

                                NOUN

know that selling friendship bracelets for $_____ each to raise money

                                       NUMBER

for the poor, sick _____ living in (the) _____ was breaking

               PLURAL NOUN   A PLACE

a school rule? That's a totally _____ rule! Serving the detention was

                            ADJECTIVE

not only humiliating—it was downright _____! I didn't know any of

                                ADJECTIVE

the other _____ in that room—but one of them smelled like rotten

         PLURAL NOUN

_____. _____ gross! And the desk I sat in had some

TYPE OF FOOD (PLURAL)   ADVERB

thick, sticky _____ substance on it that almost made me

               COLOR

_____. Then I got hit with a spit-_____ that was dripping

    VERB   NOUN

wet with _____. Disgusting! I screamed, and Mr. _____,

     TYPE OF LIQUID   CELEBRITY (MALE)

the detention monitor, gave me a nasty look. I just wanted to crawl into a hole

and _____ right then and there.

     VERB

MAD LIBS® is fun to play with friends, but you can also play it by yourself! To begin with, DO NOT look at the story on the page below. Fill in the blanks on this page with the words called for. Then, using the words you have selected, fill in the blank spaces in the story.

Now you've created your own hilarious MAD LIBS® game!

DEEPEST APOLOGIES

LAST NAME _____

ADJECTIVE _____

NOUN _____

A PLACE _____

VERB ENDING IN "ING" _____

COLOR _____

NOUN _____

PART OF THE BODY _____

VERB _____

PART OF THE BODY (PLURAL) _____

SILLY WORD _____

SAME SILLY WORD _____

ADJECTIVE _____

NOUN _____

VERB _____

PLURAL NOUN _____

NOUN _____

ADJECTIVE _____

PERSON IN ROOM (MALE) _____

MAD LIBS®
DEEPEST APOLOGIES

Dear Mrs. _____,
              LAST NAME

I am truly _____ for disrupting yesterday's class on the native
           ADJECTIVE

customs of the _____ tribes of (the) _____. It was rude
             NOUN   A PLACE

of me to burst out _____ when you explained that the tribal
               VERB ENDING IN "ING"

chief wore a/an _____-feathered headpiece in the shape of a winged
              COLOR

_____ on his _____. And my decision to
   NOUN   PART OF THE BODY

_____ in a circle with my _____ outstretched
   VERB   PART OF THE BODY (PLURAL)

while chanting "_____! _____!" was inappropriate—
             SILLY WORD   SAME SILLY WORD

even though I was only trying to mimic the _____ native dance. I
                           ADJECTIVE

understand there's a time and place for that kind of _____—and your
                        NOUN

class was not it. I know that you _____ very hard as a teacher and
                 VERB

deserve respect for teaching me and my fellow _____ every day. I hope
                 PLURAL NOUN

you accept my sincere _____ and believe I will never exercise such
           NOUN

_____ judgment again.
  ADJECTIVE

Sincerely,

_____
PERSON IN ROOM (MALE)

MAD LIBS® is fun to play with friends, but you can also play it by yourself! To begin with, DO NOT look at the story on the page below. Fill in the blanks on this page with the words called for. Then, using the words you have selected, fill in the blank spaces in the story.

Now you've created your own hilarious MAD LIBS® game!

DUNGEON DETENTION

PLURAL NOUN _____

ADJECTIVE _____

NOUN _____

PLURAL NOUN _____

ANIMAL (PLURAL) _____

TYPE OF LIQUID _____

PART OF THE BODY (PLURAL) _____

PERSON IN ROOM (MALE) _____

NOUN _____

PART OF THE BODY _____

PLURAL NOUN _____

NOUN _____

ADJECTIVE _____

ADJECTIVE _____

ADJECTIVE _____

PART OF THE BODY (PLURAL) _____

PART OF THE BODY _____

MAD LIBS
DUNGEON DETENTION

Did you know that school-age _____ were even given detentions
                                    PLURAL NOUN

back in _____ medieval times? But instead of a classroom,
            ADJECTIVE

detentions were held in an underground _____. It was pitch-black
                                             NOUN

because there were no _____ to let in sunlight. You could hear
                         PLURAL NOUN

sounds of hungry little _____ scurrying in the corners, as well as the
                          ANIMAL (PLURAL)

drip-drip-drip of _____ from the ceiling. Students were chained
                      TYPE OF LIQUID

by their _____ to the walls. Detentions were overseen by Dark
           PART OF THE BODY (PLURAL)

Lord _____. He wore a black _____ over his face,
       PERSON IN ROOM (MALE)   NOUN

and had a freakishly scarred _____ and warts all over his
                               PART OF THE BODY

abnormally large _____. Was the Dark _____ a/an
                    PLURAL NOUN   NOUN

_____ freak—or did he just dress this way to keep students on their
  ADJECTIVE

best _____ behavior? Those _____ enough to get stuck
       ADJECTIVE   ADJECTIVE

in detention with the Dark Lord fared well when they remembered these two

important tips: Keep your _____ open and your
                            PART OF THE BODY (PLURAL)

_____ shut!
  PART OF THE BODY

DETENTION DIVA

PERSON IN ROOM (FEMALE) —————————

ADJECTIVE —————————

CELEBRITY (FEMALE) —————————

PART OF THE BODY —————————

NOUN —————————

ADJECTIVE —————————

PLURAL NOUN —————————

VERB ENDING IN "ING" —————————

NOUN —————————

PERSON IN ROOM (MALE) —————————

VERB —————————

ADJECTIVE —————————

NOUN —————————

PERSON IN ROOM —————————

PLURAL NOUN —————————

TYPE OF LIQUID —————————

PART OF THE BODY —————————

ADJECTIVE —————————

MAD LIBS
DETENTION DIVA

My name is _____, and I rule this _____ school as
                  PERSON IN ROOM (FEMALE)   ADJECTIVE

the classy, sassy _____ of detention! I end up here after school more
                  CELEBRITY (FEMALE)

times than I can count on one _____! Usually my crime is
                              PART OF THE BODY

forgetting to do my _____ assignments. I mean, who has time? There
                    NOUN

are only so many hours to do other _____ things that need to get
                                   ADJECTIVE

done, like texting with my _____ or _____ online
                           PLURAL NOUN   VERB ENDING IN "ING"

or watching my favorite _____ on television. Luckily, I get a lot
                        NOUN

done in detention, too. If _____ happens to be there, I can
                          PERSON IN ROOM (MALE)

sweet-_____ him into doing my homework for me because I know
       VERB

he has a/an _____ crush on me. This other _____ named
            ADJECTIVE   NOUN

_____ will sneak out to the vending _____ and buy
PERSON IN ROOM   PLURAL NOUN

me a can of my favorite _____. And sometimes I will make
                        TYPE OF LIQUID

one of the other kids paint my _____-nails for me—just
                               PART OF THE BODY

because I can. Now that I think about it, maybe getting stuck in detention isn't

such a/an _____ thing after all!
          ADJECTIVE

MAD LIBS® is fun to play with friends, but you can also play it by yourself! To begin with, DO NOT look at the story on the page below. Fill in the blanks on this page with the words called for. Then, using the words you have selected, fill in the blank spaces in the story.

Now you've created your own hilarious MAD LIBS® game!

TEXTING, TEXTING—
THIS IS ONLY A TEXT

_____ PART OF THE BODY

_____ VERB ENDING IN "ING"

_____ PART OF THE BODY

_____ NOUN

_____ PLURAL NOUN

_____ NOUN

_____ VERB ENDING IN "ING"

_____ ADJECTIVE

_____ NOUN

_____ TYPE OF LIQUID

_____ PERSON IN ROOM

_____ PART OF THE BODY (PLURAL)

_____ VERB ENDING IN "ING"

_____ ADVERB

_____ ARTICLE OF CLOTHING

_____ TYPE OF FOOD

_____ PERSON IN ROOM

_____ PART OF THE BODY

Bored out of your _____ in detention? Well, you could do
PART OF THE BODY

some _____ or other homework, but why drain your
VERB ENDING IN "ING"

_____ when you can use your cell _____ to catch up
PART OF THE BODY   NOUN

with all your best _____ via texting?
PLURAL NOUN

JT: 'Sup, my home-_____? I'm _____ in detention
NOUN   VERB ENDING IN "ING"

right now.

Nick: UR again? What was your _____ crime this time?
ADJECTIVE

JT: I brought a squirt _____ filled with _____
NOUN   TYPE OF LIQUID

to Miss Marks's class and nailed _____ right between the
PERSON IN ROOM

_____.
PART OF THE BODY (PLURAL)

Nick: LOL! Heck, I'm downright _____ out loud at that one!
VERB ENDING IN "ING"

_____ funny stuff! What do U have up your _____
ADVERB   ARTICLE OF CLOTHING

for tomorrow?

JT: Let's just say it involves a/an _____ launcher and
TYPE OF FOOD

_____'s supersize _____.
PERSON IN ROOM   PART OF THE BODY

MAD LIBS® is fun to play with friends, but you can also play it by yourself! To begin with, DO NOT look at the story on the page below. Fill in the blanks on this page with the words called for. Then, using the words you have selected, fill in the blank spaces in the story.

Now you've created your own hilarious MAD LIBS® game!

WHO'S WHO IN DETENTION

_____ PLURAL NOUN

_____ ADJECTIVE

_____ PERSON IN ROOM (MALE)

_____ COLOR

_____ ARTICLE OF CLOTHING

_____ ADJECTIVE

_____ PLURAL NOUN

_____ PART OF THE BODY (PLURAL)

_____ PERSON IN ROOM (FEMALE)

_____ PART OF THE BODY

_____ PLURAL NOUN

_____ ADJECTIVE

_____ CELEBRITY (MALE)

_____ NOUN

_____ ADJECTIVE

_____ PART OF THE BODY (PLURAL)

MAD LIBS®
WHO'S WHO IN DETENTION

At my school, the same familiar _____ show up in detention so
                                    PLURAL NOUN

often, it's like they have formed their own _____ exclusive club.
                                                ADJECTIVE

Members include:

• _____: With his long _____ hair and his
   PERSON IN ROOM (MALE)   COLOR

tight-fitting leather _____, this dude is so ruggedly
                         ARTICLE OF CLOTHING

_____ that the female _____ in detention can't
   ADJECTIVE   PLURAL NOUN

take their _____ off him.
             PART OF THE BODY (PLURAL)

• _____: This girl has a really loud _____—
   PERSON IN ROOM (FEMALE)   PART OF THE BODY

and she knows how to use it. If she's not chewing gum and blowing

_____ in class, she's telling a teacher how mind-numbingly
   PLURAL NOUN

_____ her class is.
   ADJECTIVE

• _____: Talented at _____-ball but prone to
   CELEBRITY (MALE)   NOUN

getting into trouble, this _____ athlete spends detention
                              ADJECTIVE

flexing and admiring his muscular _____.
                                     PART OF THE BODY (PLURAL)

MAD LIBS® is fun to play with friends, but you can also play it by yourself! To begin with, DO NOT look at the story on the page below. Fill in the blanks on this page with the words called for. Then, using the words you have selected, fill in the blank spaces in the story.

Now you've created your own hilarious MAD LIBS® game!

PRANKS A LOT

ADJECTIVE

_____

ADJECTIVE

_____

PLURAL NOUN

_____

TYPE OF FOOD

_____

ANIMAL

_____

VERB ENDING IN "ING"

_____

CELEBRITY

_____

TYPE OF LIQUID

_____

PART OF THE BODY (PLURAL)

_____

VERB ENDING IN "ING"

_____

ADJECTIVE

_____

ADJECTIVE

_____

NOUN

_____

VERB ENDING IN "ING"

_____

COLOR

_____

NOUN

_____

ADJECTIVE

_____

PERSON IN ROOM

_____

MAD LIBS®
PRANKS A LOT

Nothing livens up detention quite like pulling a few _____ pranks.
ADJECTIVE

Here are some _____ ideas to get your _____ turning:
ADJECTIVE PLURAL NOUN

• Order a pepperoni-and-_____ pizza and have it delivered to
TYPE OF FOOD

detention

• Have your best friend show up dressed in a/an _____
ANIMAL

costume to perform a/an _____ telegram to your
VERB ENDING IN "ING"

favorite _____ song
CELEBRITY

• Sneak _____-filled balloons into detention and drop them
TYPE OF LIQUID

from the windows onto the _____ of unsuspecting
PART OF THE BODY (PLURAL)

students _____ below
VERB ENDING IN "ING"

• Stage a/an _____ fashion show by cranking some _____
ADJECTIVE ADJECTIVE

tunes on your i-_____ and _____ down a
NOUN VERB ENDING IN "ING"

runway formed from rows of desks

• Bring an inflatable _____-headed _____
COLOR NOUN

with you, prop it up in the chair next to you, and introduce it as your

_____ detention buddy, _____
ADJECTIVE PERSON IN ROOM

MAD LIBS® is fun to play with friends, but you can also play it by yourself! To begin with, DO NOT look at the story on the page below. Fill in the blanks on this page with the words called for. Then, using the words you have selected, fill in the blank spaces in the story.

Now you've created your own hilarious MAD LIBS® game!

DETENTION RULES

_____ ADJECTIVE

_____ PERSON IN ROOM

_____ PLURAL NOUN

_____ ADJECTIVE

_____ ADJECTIVE

_____ ADJECTIVE

_____ VERB

_____ SAME VERB

_____ PART OF THE BODY (PLURAL)

_____ A PLACE

_____ PART OF THE BODY

_____ VERB ENDING IN "ING"

_____ VERB ENDING IN "ING"

_____ ADJECTIVE

_____ NOUN

_____ PART OF THE BODY

MAD LIBS®
DETENTION RULES

A word of warning to all those who enter the _____ detention
                                                    ADJECTIVE

chambers of _____: Abide by the strict _____—or
              PERSON IN ROOM   PLURAL NOUN

suffer the _____ consequences.
            ADJECTIVE

1. Don't be late to detention. Don't be _____ or
                                              ADJECTIVE

   _____, either.
      ADJECTIVE

2. Do not _____ unless spoken to! (Tip: Even if you are spoken
              VERB

   to, it's still best not to _____!)
                                SAME VERB

3. Keep your _____ to yourself at all times.
              PART OF THE BODY (PLURAL)

4. If you need to go to the bathroom or to (the) _____, raise
                                                    A PLACE

   your _____ and ask.
          PART OF THE BODY

5. No eating or drinking! And no _____ or
                                    VERB ENDING IN "ING"

   _____, either.
      VERB ENDING IN "ING"

6. Do not make _____ noises—whether it's with a pencil,
                  ADJECTIVE

   a/an _____, or your _____!
          NOUN   PART OF THE BODY

From ESCAPE FROM DETENTION MAD LIBS® • Copyright © 2013 by Penguin Random House LLC.

MAD LIBS® is fun to play with friends, but you can also play it by yourself! To begin with, DO NOT look at the story on the page below. Fill in the blanks on this page with the words called for. Then, using the words you have selected, fill in the blank spaces in the story.

Now you've created your own hilarious MAD LIBS® game!

DETENTION SURVIVAL KIT

NOUN _____

PERSON IN ROOM _____

NOUN _____

VERB ENDING IN "ING" _____

NOUN _____

VERB _____

NOUN _____

PART OF THE BODY _____

NOUN _____

PART OF THE BODY _____

VERB _____

ADJECTIVE _____

PERSON IN ROOM _____

PERSON IN ROOM _____

NOUN _____

NOUN _____

NOUN _____

ADJECTIVE _____

My best _____, _____, is a pro at serving detentions and
　　　　　NOUN　　　　　　　PERSON IN ROOM

suggests bringing the following items to make it through the hour:

- A/An _____ phone—but don't use it for _____;
  　　　　NOUN　　　　　　　　　　　　　　　VERB ENDING IN "ING"

  instead, use it as a watch, a calculator, or a/an _____. And
  　　　　　　　　　　　　　　　　　　　　　　　　NOUN

  be sure to turn it to "_____" so it doesn't ring.
  　　　　　　　　　　VERB

- An i-_____ to listen to music. Cover up the
  　　　　NOUN

  _____-phones by wearing a hooded _____.
  PART OF THE BODY　　　　　　　　　　　　　　　NOUN

- Some tissues, in case you need to blow your _____
  　　　　　　　　　　　　　　　　　　　　　PART OF THE BODY

- Blank paper and something to _____ with. Use
  　　　　　　　　　　　　　　　VERB

  these _____ items to compose love songs to your
  　　　ADJECTIVE

  crush, _____, draw a comic strip featuring
  　　　　PERSON IN ROOM

  _____ as the underwear-wearing superhero Captain
  PERSON IN ROOM

  _____-pants, or even do something crazy, like your
  　NOUN

  _____homework
  　NOUN

- A pair of _____-glasses—you might as well look
  　　　　　NOUN

  _____ while you're there!
  　ADJECTIVE

MAD LIBS® is fun to play with friends, but you can also play it by yourself! To begin with, DO NOT look at the story on the page below. Fill in the blanks on this page with the words called for. Then, using the words you have selected, fill in the blank spaces in the story.

Now you've created your own hilarious MAD LIBS® game!

DETENTION DAYDREAMS

ADVERB _____

PART OF THE BODY _____

ADJECTIVE _____

NOUN _____

ANIMAL _____

NOUN _____

NOUN _____

PLURAL NOUN _____

NOUN _____

TYPE OF FOOD _____

NOUN _____

NOUN _____

A PLACE _____

ADJECTIVE _____

COLOR _____

PLURAL NOUN _____

PART OF THE BODY _____

ARTICLE OF CLOTHING _____

MAD LIBS®
DETENTION DAYDREAMS

Sure, you could do homework in detention, but why ruin a/an

_____ good hour taxing your _____ when
ADVERB   PART OF THE BODY

you could get lost in _____ daydreams like these:
                       ADJECTIVE

- A/An _____ in shining armor gallops up on
       NOUN

  a/an _____, shatters the window with a heavy metal
       ANIMAL

  _____, and rides off with you into the sunset
  NOUN

- A pastry chef named Le _____ wheels in a dessert cart
                         NOUN

  covered with chocolate-covered _____, _____-
                                  PLURAL NOUN   NOUN

  flavored cupcakes, and _____-stuffed pies
                         TYPE OF FOOD

- The President of the United States sends a chauffeur-driven

  _____ to bring you to the White House to advise him on
  NOUN

  how to handle the _____ crisis in (the) _____
                    NOUN   A PLACE

- _____ music fills the classroom, and suddenly you are the star
  ADJECTIVE

  of a music video, flinging around your long mane of _____
                                                      COLOR

  _____ and shaking your _____ in your
  PLURAL NOUN   PART OF THE BODY

  leopard-print _____
                ARTICLE OF CLOTHING

MAD LIBS® is fun to play with friends, but you can also play it by yourself! To begin with, DO NOT look at the story on the page below. Fill in the blanks on this page with the words called for. Then, using the words you have selected, fill in the blank spaces in the story.

Now you've created your own hilarious MAD LIBS® game!

THE DETENTION SONG

EXCLAMATION _____

SAME EXCLAMATION _____

ADJECTIVE _____

VERB ENDING IN "ING" _____

ADVERB _____

ADJECTIVE _____

NOUN _____

ADJECTIVE _____

PERSON IN ROOM _____

ADJECTIVE _____

ANIMAL _____

NOUN _____

PART OF THE BODY (PLURAL) _____

ADJECTIVE _____

TYPE OF LIQUID _____

VERB ENDING IN "ING" _____

MAD LIBS®
THE DETENTION SONG

_____! _____! I'm once again stuck
  EXCLAMATION   SAME EXCLAMATION

In detention—it's due to my own _____ luck!
                      ADJECTIVE

I'm _____ here 'cuz I was _____ wrong,
   VERB ENDING IN "ING"   ADVERB

And I'm singing this _____ detention song!
                 ADJECTIVE

Woe is me! I'm a/an _____! I'm in some _____ trouble
              NOUN   ADJECTIVE

For calling _____ a/an _____ _____
        PERSON IN ROOM   ADJECTIVE   ANIMAL

—but it was my double!

Now I'm chained to this _____ when I just want to flee!
                   NOUN

Woe is me! Woe is me! Woe is me!

I can twiddle my _____—but that's not much fun.
           PART OF THE BODY (PLURAL)

How soon until this _____ detention is done?!
               ADJECTIVE

Wish I had some flavored _____ to drown all my sorrows—
                  TYPE OF LIQUID

I hope I won't be _____ in detention tomorrow!
         VERB ENDING IN "ING"

DETENTION DUTIES

VERB ENDING IN "ING" _____

VERB _____

ADJECTIVE _____

PLURAL NOUN _____

ADJECTIVE _____

NOUN _____

ADVERB _____

ADJECTIVE _____

PLURAL NOUN _____

TYPE OF LIQUID _____

PLURAL NOUN _____

ADVERB _____

TYPE OF LIQUID _____

CELEBRITY (MALE) _____

PLURAL NOUN _____

ADJECTIVE _____

EXCLAMATION _____

PART OF THE BODY _____

MAD LIBS® is fun to play with friends, but you can also play it by yourself! To begin with, DO NOT look at the story on the page below. Fill in the blanks on this page with the words called for. Then, using the words you have selected, fill in the blank spaces in the story.

Now you've created your own hilarious MAD LIBS® game!

MAD LIBS
DETENTION DUTIES

At our school, detentions don't involve _____ in a classroom
VERB ENDING IN "ING"

for an hour. Instead, the principal makes us _____ around the
VERB

school. First we head to the cafeteria and help the _____ lunch ladies
ADJECTIVE

clean up. We have to sweep the _____ and scrape crusty,
PLURAL NOUN

_____ tater tots and cheesy, _____-topped pizza off the
ADJECTIVE ... *NOUN*

tabletops. It's _____ nasty! Next we go to every _____
ADVERB ... *ADJECTIVE*

classroom and empty the waste-_____. Then we fill buckets with
PLURAL NOUN

_____ and wipe down the chalk-_____ until they are
TYPE OF LIQUID ... *PLURAL NOUN*

_____ clean! But the worst job of all is mopping up the spit, sweat,
ADVERB

and _____ in the locker rooms. If our gym teacher, _____,
TYPE OF LIQUID ... *CELEBRITY (MALE)*

is there, he makes us go through the lockers and remove all the stinky gym

_____ and _____ underpants crammed in there.
PLURAL NOUN ... *ADJECTIVE*

_____! The smell alone makes me sick to my _____!
EXCLAMATION ... *PART OF THE BODY*

MAD LIBS® is fun to play with friends, but you can also play it by yourself! To begin with, DO NOT look at the story on the page below. Fill in the blanks on this page with the words called for. Then, using the words you have selected, fill in the blank spaces in the story.

Now you've created your own hilarious MAD LIBS® game!

NOTICE TO PARENTS

LAST NAME _____

ADJECTIVE _____

PERSON IN ROOM (MALE) _____

PLURAL NOUN _____

CELEBRITY (FEMALE) _____

PART OF THE BODY _____

PLURAL NOUN _____

PART OF THE BODY _____

NOUN _____

VERB _____

PART OF THE BODY _____

ADJECTIVE _____

ADJECTIVE _____

NUMBER _____

A PLACE _____

NOUN _____

VERB _____

PERSON IN ROOM _____

MAD LIBS®
NOTICE TO PARENTS

Dear Mr. and Mrs. _____:

LAST NAME

I am writing to inform you of yet another troubling and _____

ADJECTIVE

incident involving your son, _____. Today he was juggling

PERSON IN ROOM (MALE)

_____ in the hallway when one went flying out of his hands and hit

PLURAL NOUN

the science teacher, Miss _____, in the _____ and

CELEBRITY (FEMALE) ... PART OF THE BODY

knocked her down a flight of _____. She suffered a broken

PLURAL NOUN

_____ and a bruised _____, and worst of all, she may

PART OF THE BODY ... NOUN

never _____ again! I'm not sure what goes through your son's

VERB

_____ when he decides to pull _____ stunts like this.

PART OF THE BODY ... ADJECTIVE

Is everything _____ at home? As a result of his actions, I had to give

ADJECTIVE

him another _____ detentions to serve. The next time, he will be

NUMBER

kicked out of (the) _____. I would like to schedule a

A PLACE

parent-_____ conference with you to discuss our next steps. Please

NOUN

_____ at your earliest convenience.

VERB

Sincerely,

Principal _____

PERSON IN ROOM

MAD LIBS® is fun to play with friends, but you can also play it by yourself! To begin with, DO NOT look at the story on the page below. Fill in the blanks on this page with the words called for. Then, using the words you have selected, fill in the blank spaces in the story.

Now you've created your own hilarious MAD LIBS® game!

¡TRAPPED IN DETENTION

PERSON IN ROOM_____

NOUN_____

ADVERB_____

PLURAL NOUN_____

NUMBER_____

TYPE OF FOOD (PLURAL)_____

ADJECTIVE_____

NOUN_____

PLURAL NOUN_____

VERB ENDING IN "ING"_____

PART OF THE BODY (PLURAL)_____

TYPE OF LIQUID_____

PLURAL NOUN_____

PART OF THE BODY_____

ANIMAL (PLURAL)_____

ADJECTIVE_____

CELEBRITY_____

ADJECTIVE_____

MAD LIBS®
¡TRAPPED IN DETENTION

My BFF, _____, and I host our own web show called
                    PERSON IN ROOM

i-_____. It's _____ popular among today's young
      NOUN   ADVERB

_____; in fact, more than _____ people tune in weekly to
  PLURAL NOUN   NUMBER

watch us. Today we are doing our show live from detention. We have to be

careful that Mr. von _____, the detention monitor, doesn't
                     TYPE OF FOOD (PLURAL)

catch us—or we'll be in very _____ water! Luckily he spends most
                              ADJECTIVE

of detention in the _____'s lounge grading _____. We
                         NOUN   PLURAL NOUN

start the web show by doing a little random _____ to loosen up
                                            VERB ENDING IN "ING"

our _____. Then everyone in the room works together with
    PART OF THE BODY (PLURAL)

bottles of _____ and pieces of _____ to make the world's
           TYPE OF LIQUID   PLURAL NOUN

largest spitball—which we promptly hurl at the _____ of the
                                               PART OF THE BODY

kid sleeping at the back of the room. Lastly, we "borrow" the two albino

_____ from the science lab for a/an _____ race—the one
ANIMAL (PLURAL)   ADJECTIVE

named _____ won! Who says detention is a bad thing? Frankly, I
      CELEBRITY

found it to be pretty darn _____!
                           ADJECTIVE

MAD LIBS® is fun to play with friends, but you can also play it by yourself! To begin with, DO NOT look at the story on the page below. Fill in the blanks on this page with the words called for. Then, using the words you have selected, fill in the blank spaces in the story.

Now you've created your own hilarious MAD LIBS® game!

YOUR MOTHER AND I MET IN DETENTION

_____ PLURAL NOUN

_____ ADJECTIVE

_____ NOUN

_____ NOUN

_____ PERSON IN ROOM (FEMALE)

_____ ADJECTIVE

_____ VERB (PAST TENSE)

_____ NOUN

_____ PART OF THE BODY (PLURAL)

_____ NOUN

_____ PLURAL NOUN

_____ NOUN

_____ PART OF THE BODY

_____ ADVERB

_____ ADJECTIVE

_____ ADVERB

_____ PERSON IN ROOM (MALE)

I was going through some of my parents' old school _____ when I came
                                                    PLURAL NOUN

across this _____ letter from my dad proclaiming his love for my
            ADJECTIVE

_____—whom he met in detention of all places!
NOUN

To the _____ of my dreams, _____:
       NOUN   PERSON IN ROOM (FEMALE)

My _____ world turned upside down the day you _____
   ADJECTIVE   VERB (PAST TENSE)

in detention with me. I had never seen a prettier _____ before.
                                                   NOUN

When you sat there with your _____ folded so daintily on
                             PART OF THE BODY (PLURAL)

the desk, I remember thinking, This is one classy _____. She's not
                                                   NOUN

like the other _____! And that's when I knew I had to get your
               PLURAL NOUN

attention. Looking back, perhaps folding a paper _____-ball and
                                                 NOUN

flicking it at your _____ was not the way to go. Please
                    PART OF THE BODY

understand I was _____ nervous. I mean, it's not every day that you
                 ADVERB

meet the person you want to grow _____ with.
                                 ADJECTIVE

Truly, madly, _____ in love with you,
              ADVERB

_____
PERSON IN ROOM (MALE)

MAD LIBS® is fun to play with friends, but you can also play it by yourself! To begin with, DO NOT look at the story on the page below. Fill in the blanks on this page with the words called for. Then, using the words you have selected, fill in the blank spaces in the story.

Now you've created your own hilarious MAD LIBS® game!

ESCAPE PLAN

PART OF THE BODY _____

NOUN _____

PLURAL NOUN _____

PERSON IN ROOM (MALE) _____

ADJECTIVE _____

PART OF THE BODY (PLURAL) _____

EXCLAMATION _____

NOUN _____

NOUN _____

TYPE OF LIQUID _____

ADJECTIVE _____

ARTICLE OF CLOTHING (PLURAL) _____

NOUN _____

NOUN _____

ADVERB _____

VERB _____

MAD LIBS®
ESCAPE PLAN

No one in their right _____ wants to be in detention, so you
PART OF THE BODY

should always have an escape plan in your back _____. Here are
NOUN

step-by-step _____ for one:
PLURAL NOUN

1. Become friends with someone like _____, who
PERSON IN ROOM (MALE)

is mechanically _____ and can do anything with his
ADJECTIVE

_____.
PART OF THE BODY (PLURAL)

2. Once detention starts, have someone run into the classroom and yell

to the teacher, "_____! There's a/an _____ on fire
EXCLAMATION   NOUN

in the boys' locker room!"

3. As soon as the teacher gets there, have your friend activate the

_____ sprinklers and douse the teacher with
NOUN

_____ so she is soaking _____.
TYPE OF LIQUID   ADJECTIVE

4. Now that the teacher is out of the picture, grab all the

_____ from the lockers and tie them together to
ARTICLE OF CLOTHING (PLURAL)

form a/an _____ ladder.
NOUN

5. Climb down to the _____ below.
NOUN

6. You're _____ free! Now _____ for your life!
ADVERB   VERB

MAD LIBS® is fun to play with friends, but you can also play it by yourself! To begin with, DO NOT look at the story on the page below. Fill in the blanks on this page with the words called for. Then, using the words you have selected, fill in the blank spaces in the story.

Now you've created your own hilarious MAD LIBS® game!

EXCUSES FOR WHY YOU MISSED DETENTION

ADJECTIVE _____

NOUN _____

ANIMAL _____

PART OF THE BODY _____

COLOR _____

PART OF THE BODY _____

PLURAL NOUN _____

NUMBER _____

PLURAL NOUN _____

ADJECTIVE _____

CELEBRITY (MALE) _____

NOUN _____

ARTICLE OF CLOTHING _____

NOUN _____

ANIMAL _____

PLURAL NOUN _____

NOUN _____

MAD LIBS®
EXCUSES FOR WHY YOU MISSED DETENTION

So many detentions, so little time! Need a/an _____ reason that you
ADJECTIVE

couldn't show up today? Here are some excuses:

- I had a note from my _____, but my _____ ate it.
  NOUN   ANIMAL

- I had a sore _____ and _____ bumps
  PART OF THE BODY   COLOR

  all over my _____ and didn't want the other
  PART OF THE BODY

  _____ to catch it.
  PLURAL NOUN

- I was on my way when _____ little green _____ took me
  NUMBER   PLURAL NOUN

  back to their spaceship to perform _____ experiments on me.
  ADJECTIVE

- _____ called and asked if I could be a/an _____
  CELEBRITY (MALE)   NOUN

  in his next movie.

- My _____ clashed with the _____ that
  ARTICLE OF CLOTHING   NOUN

  the teacher was wearing.

- A/An _____ escaped from the zoo, and I had to stop it
  ANIMAL

  before it trampled all the _____ in the city.
  PLURAL NOUN

- I noticed how long the _____ had grown on school grounds
  NOUN

  and decided to mow it.

MAD LIBS® is fun to play with friends, but you can also play it by yourself! To begin with, DO NOT look at the story on the page below. Fill in the blanks on this page with the words called for. Then, using the words you have selected, fill in the blank spaces in the story.

Now you've created your own hilarious MAD LIBS® game!

DETENTION-GETTER
RECORD SETTER

_____ ADJECTIVE

_____ NUMBER

_____ NOUN

_____ PERSON IN ROOM

_____ ADJECTIVE

_____ PERSON IN ROOM

_____ PLURAL NOUN

_____ ADJECTIVE

_____ PART OF THE BODY (PLURAL)

_____ ADJECTIVE

_____ PERSON IN ROOM

_____ NOUN

_____ PERSON IN ROOM

_____ NOUN

_____ ADJECTIVE

_____ NOUN

_____ PART OF THE BODY

Nate Nastygram set a/an _____ record this year with _____
ADJECTIVE   NUMBER

detentions earned—more than any other _____ in Ridgeway
                                                    NOUN

School's history! _____, a reporter for the school yearbook, talked
                  PERSON IN ROOM

to him about his _____ achievement:
                 ADJECTIVE

Reporter: How does it feel to have broken _____'s long-standing
                                              PERSON IN ROOM

record for most _____ earned?
                PLURAL NOUN

Nate: Well, it feels like a/an _____ weight has been lifted off my
                                   ADJECTIVE

_____ now that I actually did it. I mean, how awesome and
PART OF THE BODY (PLURAL)

_____ am I?
ADJECTIVE

Reporter: Yep, you're right up there with _____, who won the most
                                              PERSON IN ROOM

_____-ball games, and _____, who got the highest
NOUN   PERSON IN ROOM

_____ scores out of the whole class.
NOUN

Nate: So do I get a/an _____ award for my achievement—a trophy
                          ADJECTIVE

or a medal or a/an _____?
                   NOUN

Reporter: Nope, sorry—just your handsome _____ pictured in
                                             PART OF THE BODY

the yearbook.

DETENTION MOVIES

_____ PLURAL NOUN

_____ ADJECTIVE

_____ COLOR

_____ PLURAL NOUN

_____ PERSON IN ROOM (FEMALE)

_____ NOUN

_____ NUMBER

_____ ADJECTIVE

_____ NOUN

_____ PERSON IN ROOM

_____ PLURAL NOUN

_____ ADJECTIVE

_____ PERSON IN ROOM

_____ VERB

_____ NOUN

_____ PLURAL NOUN

_____ PART OF THE BODY

MAD LIBS® is fun to play with friends, but you can also play it by yourself! To begin with, DO NOT look at the story on the page below. Fill in the blanks on this page with the words called for. Then, using the words you have selected, fill in the blank spaces in the story.

Now you've created your own hilarious MAD LIBS® game!

MAD LIBS®
DETENTION MOVIES

Grab a bucket of hot buttered _____ and settle in for a viewing of

PLURAL NOUN

_____ movies about detention.

ADJECTIVE

- *Ninjas in Detention*: The _____-clad _____

COLOR   PLURAL NOUN

  who gather in detention every day are really a secret society of ninjas

  who protect the school from trouble. The sweet old principal, Ms.

  _____, is their martial-arts master.

PERSON IN ROOM (FEMALE)

- *The* _____ *Club*: _____ kids—including

NOUN   NUMBER

  a/an _____ athlete, a highly intelligent _____,

ADJECTIVE   NOUN

  and a troublemaker named _____—gather for a Saturday

PERSON IN ROOM

  detention and learn that while they hang out with different types of

  _____, they are actually more _____ than

PLURAL NOUN   ADJECTIVE

  they thought.

- _____ *Blart: Detention Cop*: This _____-out-

PERSON IN ROOM   VERB

  loud comedy is about an overweight _____ whose job is to

NOUN

  watch over the rebellious _____ in detention armed only

PLURAL NOUN

  with his wits, a pair of _____-cuffs, and some duct

PART OF THE BODY

  tape.

Download Mad Libs today!

Join the millions of Mad Libs fans creating wacky and wonderful stories on our apps!